SECURING
YOUR CHILD'S FUTURE

SECURING

YOUR CHILD'S FUTURE

A Financial and Legal Planner
for Parents

Winifred Conkling

Fawcett Columbine

NEW YORK

A Fawcett Columbine Book
Published by Ballantine Books

Copyright © 1994 by Winifred Conkling

Foreword copyright © 1994 by Peter Passell

Library of Congress Catalog Card Number: 94-94642

ISBN: 0-449-90876-3

Cover design by Judy Herbstman
Cover photo © Michael Keller/FPG International
Text design and composition by John Reinhardt

Manufactured in the United States of America

First Edition: January 1995

10 9 8 7 6 5 4 3 2 1

For Hannah Pamelia Rak
My inspiration and my joy

CONTENTS

ACKNOWLEDGMENTS

A book, like a baby, benefits from the love, support, and constructive criticism offered by a lot of different people. Special thanks to:

My husband, Jonathan Rak, who is both an exemplary daddy and a fine copy editor; Elise Howard, my friend, my colleague, and Tristan's mom, who nurtured this project from its conception;

Alexia Dorszynski, who crossed my T's and dotted my I's (and understood when I couldn't meet a deadline because my baby was cutting two molars and needed extra hugs);

Those "parent testers" who helped to shape the manuscript, including: Pam and Sam Abutaleb, Attison and Karen Barnes, Mandy and Mark Bolgiano, Melise Blakeslee, Bill Carter, Jack and Suzy Coffey, Duncan and Susan Blair, Andrew and Kathryn Blair, Connie and Tim Prigg, Jack and Sue Rust, Beth and Rip Sullivan, and Kathy and Mike Zupan;

Ballantine editors Joëlle Delbourgo and Phebe Kirkham, who saw the need for this book and offered intelligent and insightful suggestions for its development at every stage;

Paul Matarazzo, art director, and John Reinhardt, designer, who translated a complicated manuscript full of charts, subheads, and sidebars into its final accessible and appealing form.

Karen Clark, who meticulously checked every phone number and address in this book and is largely responsible for its ultimate accuracy.

FOREWORD

by Peter Passell, *New York Times* Financial Columnist

As a loving, caring, feeling parent, you've read all the right stuff about child care. If little Jessica wakes up with red spots on her belly, it must be chicken pox. Or is it an allergy? And is she likely to give it to the kids at Cousin Zeke's birthday party next Saturday? Never mind: the answer must be on page 349 of Penelope Leach. If it isn't, that infinitely patient nurse in Dr. Whoosit's office is sure to have the definitive word.

You are equally prepared to help your child negotiate the social and emotional potholes along the road to maturity. You know what to say to Jessica when she beans her nursery school mate with a Fisher-Price hook-and-ladder set—and perhaps even what to tell Jessica's teacher when she does it a second time. And then there's Jessica's older brother, Jason, who is learning to "just say no" in the fifth grade. The pamphlet they sent home with his report card offers handy tips on how to respond when Jason wonders why you always have a Dewar's before dinner and a Marlboro after. . . .

But do you know how to pick a guardian for Jess and Jason, in case Mom and Dad are hit by a bolt of lightning? And do you know how much life insurance it would take to tide them through without parents around to pick up the bills?

Of course, lightning rarely strikes, but taxes do—quite regularly. Is there a way to get Washington to pay for part of Jessica's day care or

Jason's braces? For that matter, is there a way to start saving now for their tuition at Old RahRah U. without having to turn over a quarter of your hard-won dollars to the Internal Revenue Service?

Truth is, today's parents are overwhelmed with information on feeding, clothing, and medicating their children, not to mention coping with their toilet-training, reading skills, and sex lives. But for reasons that elude me, the basics of planning for kids' legal and financial futures must be scrounged from the occasional article in *Money* and *Kiplinger's* magazines, or the odd chapter in general guides to personal law and finance. That's where Winifred Conkling's splendid manual, *Securing Your Child's Future: A Financial and Legal Planner for Parents* fits in.

Conkling is uniquely qualified to fill the gap. As a former editor for *Consumer Reports* she understands what ordinary people who must make ordinary financial and legal decisions ought to know. As a demon researcher, she has relentlessly tracked down the information and organized it in painless-to-use form. And as a mother of a two-year-old (an angel, naturally, named Hannah), her stake in the book's accuracy and good sense goes beyond standard pride in authorship.

Each of the chapters begins with the nuts and bolts, a few chatty pages outlining what you need to think about. For example, "Beyond the ID Bracelet" explains how to obtain a birth certificate and a social security number and how to enroll the baby in your health insurance plan. "Great Expectations" expounds on the choice of an obstetrician or midwife, hospital or birthing center, and offers a checklist of expenses that may need to be covered out of pocket. In "Economics 101" she offers a primer on investing bonds, mutual funds, annuities and (often overlooked) building equity in a home.

As important, the author doesn't leave you dangling with a few abstract tips and no advice on how to apply them beyond the usual breezy recommendation to hire a good physician, lawyer or accountant. The chapter "Securing Your Family's Future" provides the names and telephone numbers of four companies that will list the half-dozen cheapest policies among hundreds monitored by the services. "Great Expectations" lists the average charges for both vaginal and cesarean deliveries in each of four regions of the country, as well as the names and sources of a dozen reliable books and pamphlets on shopping for medical care. "Your Will Be Done" offers a state-by-state listing of the acceptability of handwritten wills.

Last but hardly least, Conkling provides detailed advice on how to maintain records, and what to do, month-by-month, to ensure a smooth transition to parenthood.

As an economist and journalist, I have grown jaded to promises of how-to books that will solve every problem in twelve easy steps. *Securing Your Child's Future: A Financial and Legal Planner for Parents* is a refreshing contrast. No hype, no razzle-dazzle; just the solid, workaday information you need to clear the way for what should be the greatest event of your life.

INTRODUCTION

You'd do anything for your children. You'd stay up all night pacing the floor to comfort them; you'd go to the grocery store at 2 A.M. to buy disposable diapers for them. Without hesitation you'd sit through piano recitals, watch endless reruns of "Sesame Street," and coach a losing Little League team.

But have you done all you can to prepare for their future? Have you written a will, selected a guardian, and purchased life and disability insurance? Have you arranged for appropriate and affordable child care, budgeted for the inevitable costs of raising a child, and started planning how to pay those first college tuition bills?

Being a responsible parent and loving your children requires more than cuddles and comfort and kind words. It also includes providing for their future financial security and dealing with the unpleasant possibility that you might not always be able to be there for them.

These are not easy issues to deal with intellectually or emotionally, but this book will help. It's divided into two parts—legal matters and money matters—though some subjects, such as estate planning, actually involve both legal and financial issues. The book is further divided into chapters, complete with worksheets and checklists of issues you need to consider and decisions you need to make.

Of course, this single volume can't answer all your questions or cover all your planning needs. But the Resources section of each chapter will help guide you toward organizations, books, and other references that should provide more-detailed information.

Whether you're expecting your first child or are already the parent of six, this book has something for you. If you're waiting for the stork to arrive, the timetable in the appendix will help you plan how to accomplish the necessary tasks before your due date. If you're already a parent, the work sheets and step-by-step checklists will help you accomplish your goals between diaper changes and midnight feedings. Remember, it's never too late—or too early—to start planning.

PART 1

LEGAL MATTERS

UNLESS YOU'RE MARRIED TO A LAWYER, legal advice isn't cheap. But in the long run it usually pays to consult a legal expert when you want to get your affairs in order.

Writing a will and selecting a guardian are two of the most important things you can do for your child—and among the easiest tasks to put off or overlook. Most people don't like thinking about the possibility of not being there to watch their children grow up, but the fact is, spending a few hours planning for the unexpected can save your children a lot of heartache and expense.

Adoptive, surrogate, and single parents face additional challenges that make it still more critical that they plan ahead. Whether or not you are part of a traditional family, only by preparing appropriate legal documents can you be sure that your instructions will be followed.

In addition to wrestling with the big questions, you will have to deal with the everyday legal hassles of birth certificates, insurance claims, and Social Security numbers. Filling out forms and filing claims can be trying, but the paperwork burden of becoming a parent won't seem so intimidating once you understand the rules.

CHAPTER 1

YOUR WILL BE DONE

Getting Your Estate in Order

NUTS AND BOLTS

If you haven't written a will, now's the time to do it. You owe it to your children to take steps to provide for their financial and emotional needs if you die. Besides, if you can't take it with you, you might as well make sure your children—not Uncle Sam—get it when you go.

If you're among the two out of three Americans who don't have a will, you're effectively leaving it up to a judge in probate court to divvy up your goods according to the laws of the state where you live. Such one-size-fits-all laws are impersonal and inflexible—and can be unsuitable for your family's needs. In most states if you die intestate, or without a will, a prescribed pecking order of priority for inheritance automatically kicks in: first your surviving spouse and children inherit, then your parents, then your brothers and sisters, then your nieces and nephews. If you have no legal heirs, your estate will escheat, or pass to the state.

Without a will the court must follow the letter of the law, regardless of the emotional and financial consequences to your survivors. Without a will family heirlooms may have to be sold to divide your estate as the law prescribes. Without a will your friends and favorite charities go empty-handed. Without a will you won't be able to provide for a domestic partner if you aren't married. In some cases, if you die without a will your children can end up shortchanged. For example, if you've divorced and remarried and have children from your first marriage, in some states your current spouse could inherit everything, leaving your children with nothing.

Even if you have no real gripes with how the state would divide your estate, you can't be sure that the judge would name an appropriate guardian for your child. Ideally you would write your will before the child arrives, either by birth or adoption. But even if you have an older child, it's probably time to write a will or to update the one you have.

GETTING STARTED

Your last will and testament describes how you want your worldly possessions divided and who you want to handle your financial and personal affairs when you die. The document opens with a section identifying you, stating that the document is a will, and revoking all previous wills. After that your will:

■ **Names an executor**. The executor (who may be called a personal representative in some states) is the person responsible for settling your affairs. The job can be relatively simple or quite complex, depending on how complicated your financial affairs happen to be.

In general, the executor's job description includes:

- Taking an inventory of your property;
- Paying your debts, funeral expenses, and taxes;
- Selling your property, if necessary, to cover your debts;
- Distributing your property according to your will; and
- Submitting a final accounting to your heirs and in some states to the probate court.

If you don't have a will, the probate court, which is responsible for overseeing the execution of your will, appoints an administrator to do the job. The administrator can be either an individual or an institution, such as a bank or trust company. Both are able to charge a fee for their services, but you can be sure that the bank will collect the highest-allowable fee. Typically the fees are 5 percent on the first $100,000, 4 percent on the next $200,000, 3 percent on the next $700,000, and so forth.

All executors appointed in a will—even family members—have the right to be paid for the work required in settling the estate. Reasonable compensation in most states is defined as 3 to 5 percent of the value of the estate. Many people choose to name a major beneficiary as executor to keep the money all in the family.

When selecting an executor (or executrix, a female executor), look for someone who is capable, of legal age, respected by your family, and not much older than you are so that he or she won't be likely to die before you do. It's usually easier to have an executor who lives in your state, but it's not required. You don't have to search the family tree for an economics major or a financial whiz: most adults should have little difficulty settling a simple estate. To avoid offending a relative and to share the burden, some people name co-executors. Many people name their adult children as co-executors, especially when the estate is to be divided between them.

Naturally it's wise to discuss the job with the person you'd like to appoint to make sure he or she is willing. It's wise also to appoint an alternate executor in case your first choice is unable or unwilling to serve.

Unless your will states otherwise, the executor is usually required by law to post bond. In essence the bond is insurance to protect your heirs against the executor's absconding with your money or property. The premium for the bond often is 1 percent of the value of the property being managed; for example, $5,000 for a $500,000 estate. Since you're going to appoint a trustworthy person, you can save your heir a needless expense by including in your will a sentence waiving bond.

■ **Names a guardian for your minor children**. See Chapter 2.

■ **Leaves gifts**. Just as toddlers fight over their toys, grownups fight over the family heirlooms in far too many cases. You can put an end to a lot of the bickering by leaving property as *specific gifts*—"I leave my great-grandmother Pamelia's diamond starburst pin to my sister, Joan"—or as *general gifts*—"I leave $10,000 to my brother, Fred." Specific gifts come from the property of your estate, general gifts from the estate's general assets.

Your will needs to cover every contingency. You should indicate what you want to have happen to the gifts if the beneficiary doesn't outlive you. And you must also state what you want done if specific items are no longer in your estate when you die. The general rule is that the person who is supposed to inherit an object that is no longer part of the estate is simply out of luck, but you can also state that you would like the person to receive a substitute item or the cash value.

When making specific gifts, be as specific as possible. Describe the item in detail so that there's no confusion over which necklace or which grandmother's pearl earrings. Don't mention "my aunt Elise's necklace"; refer instead to "my aunt Elise's 18-inch pearl necklace with the diamond clasp."

If you don't want to go to the trouble of making specific gifts in your will, you can write a letter to your executor indicating how you would like your personal items distributed. Keep in mind, however, that such a letter isn't legally binding.

■ **Divides what's left over**. Your residuary estate is all the property you haven't specifically mentioned elsewhere in your will. You must state how you would like this divided among your heirs.

Since it's impossible to know now what your estate will be worth when you die, it's best to divide your residuary estate as fractions or percentages of the estate rather than as specific sums. If your $50,000 nest egg grows to $250,000 between the time you write your will and the time it takes effect, your children will be mighty disappointed to learn that they will be receiving a small sum allotted from the earlier, smaller estate. In the same way you can create problems for your heirs if your savings shrink from $250,000 to $50,000 and your will specifies a gift of $25,000 to a favorite charity. Your intention may have been to donate one-tenth of your estate to charity, but in fact you will have given away half of your children's inheritance. Use a specific gift only if you want to limit or guarantee a gift to an heir.

Even if your kids are in diapers, you should consider the way you might want your assets distributed to your grandchildren. (You should update your will periodically, of course, but far too many people never bother to revise it as circumstances change.) Do you want your grand-children to inherit equally? Or do you want your children to inherit equally, regardless of how many children they have? The choices you make in your will today will have an impact on your children's children.

■ **Provides guidelines for paying taxes and other expenses**. How do you want your taxes and expenses paid? If you have any prefer-ences—if you'd rather have the executor sell stock than your great-grandfather's gold pocket watch to raise the cash—this is the place to say so.

■ **States the executor's options**. In one section of your will you give the executor the right to sell or dispose of your property in order to execute your will. You can also restrict the executor in this regard by saying the executor should not sell off the specific gifts. Be aware, though, that if there isn't enough cash to cover the taxes, the property may have to be sold anyway.

AGAINST YOUR WILL

Even if you write a will, you're not entirely free to decide who gets what after you're gone. In most states your current spouse can claim a minimum share—typically one-third to one-half of your estate—unless he or she has signed a prenuptial agreement specifying otherwise. This so-called elective share is the right of your spouse, who can go to court and demand it.

Let's say you give your spouse 30 percent of your estate in your will and the state law says that your spouse is entitled to a minimum of 50 percent. If your spouse challenges the will, the probate court *must* override your wishes and award the money.

If you are separated, divorced, or living with a significant other, check your state's laws about elective share. Most states revoke an ex-spouse's right of inheritance after divorce, but not after separation. Some states provide no inheritance rights to people who are not legal-ly married; others consider a couple legally wed in a "common-law" marriage, even though no formal marriage ceremony has taken place, if they live together as husband and wife for a stated period. States that currently recognize common-law marriage are Alabama, Colorado, Georgia, Idaho, Iowa, Kansas, Montana, Ohio, Oklahoma, Pennsylvania, Rhode Island, South Carolina, Texas, and the District of Columbia. No state provides an elective share to a same-sex partner; the only way to provide for a partner in such cases is to write a will.

Though you can't disinherit your spouse, in every state but Louisiana you can disinherit your children. If you wish to write your kids out of the will, it's best to mention them by name to show that you did not simply forget them. In many states if you don't specifically mention the disinherited heirs by name, the court assumes that it was an oversight and includes these forgotten heirs in the final distribution. Many people choose to make their intentions clear by awarding these would-be heirs the tidy sum of one dollar. You might also write a letter to your executor explaining your reasons for disinheriting the person. (You don't want to include the remarks in the will because your disinherited heirs may contest the will—or worse yet, sue your estate for libel.)

If you so desire, you can nag your children from the grave. In your will you can state certain conditions under which your heirs can inherit. For example, you can set up a trust and stipulate that your daughter can't get her hands on the money until she attends a stop-smoking clinic or that your son can't collect until he graduates from college.

CHANGING YOUR MIND

If you change your mind about what's in your will, you can revoke it at any time. All you have to do is write a new will and state that all previous wills are revoked.

Sometimes the changes you want to make aren't worthy of redrafting the entire document. In such cases you can add a written amendment, or codicil (Latin for "little will"). There's no limit to the number of codicils you can add, but each must be properly witnessed. And if you make several changes, it's probably best to draft a new will to avoid confusion. Never try to change your will by writing on the original; that may invalidate the entire document.

Review your will every few years to make sure it still does what you'd like it to do. You will probably have to write several wills in your lifetime. As a rule it's time to update your will if any of the following takes place:

- The birth or adoption of a child or grandchild;
- The death of a beneficiary or a named executor;
- Marriage or divorce;

- A major change in the state or federal estate or tax laws;
- A significant change in your financial status;
- A major change in the health-care needs of someone in your family;
- A change in the personal or financial situation of your named guardian; or
- A move to another state.

DO YOU NEED A LAWYER?

Lawyers have been called the "hidden heir" in most estates because of the high cost of writing wills and probating estates. Indeed, lawyers are expensive. However, though most lawyers bill by the hour—at rates that can exceed $100 an hour—many charge a flat fee for writing a will. The fee may run anywhere from $100 for a simple will to several thousand dollars for a complete estate-planning package.

No-frills wills that you prepare yourself using a standard format are valid if they have all the necessary information and are properly executed. Preprinted or computer-generated, fill-in-the-blank wills, also called statutory wills, serve the needs of many people but restrict your options in leaving property, so they may not be right for you if you have an unusual arrangement or wishes.

When it comes to writing a will, there are no fixed rules about when you should consult a lawyer and when you can do the job yourself. But you should almost certainly seek a lawyer's help in the following situations:

- If your estate is worth more than $600,000. This is the amount that can trigger the federal estate tax (see page 13). Though your estate can pass to your spouse tax-free, the money will be taxed when your spouse dies unless certain steps are taken to avoid the tax;
- If you want to set up a trust;
- If you plan to disinherit someone. You'll want to make sure your will is invulnerable in case it is challenged by the disinherited person;
- If one of your beneficiaries needs special care; or
- If you own a business or have complicated property arrangements.

You may be able to cut down on a lawyer's fee by doing some home-work. Before making an appointment, draft a sample will. If you don't want to take the time to draw up a first draft of your will, at least esti-mate your net worth and make tentative decisions about beneficiaries, guardians, and executors.

PASSING BY PROBATE

Probate literally means "proving the will." A probate court (called a chancery court or surrogate's court in some states) is the court that supervises the distribution of your wealth after you die. Your estate goes through probate whether you have a will or not.

In general, it's to your heirs' advantage to have as much of your estate as possible pass to them directly, without going through pro-bate. Though some states have streamlined procedures for small estates, the probate procedures can easily take nine months to two years to complete, depending on the complexity of the will, the num-ber of beneficiaries, and the value of the estate.

You probably can't avoid probate entirely, but you may be able to minimize the share of your estate that passes through probate. There are four basic ways to avoid probate by passing property outside a will: gifts, insurance benefits, joint property ownership, and trusts.

Gifts

You can avoid probate by simply giving your things away before you die. There are limits, however. Each year you can give away up to $10,000 per person to any number of people tax-free. There are no limits on gifts between spouses. If your spouse wants to give a joint gift, you can double your generosity and give up to $20,000 a year tax-free. After that you start to incur gift taxes, which are levied on you, the giver, not the recipient. There is one exception: You don't have to pay the gift tax if the money is used to pay someone's medical or educational bills, no matter how much money is involved. To qual-ify for the exclusion, though, you have to pay the bill directly; that is, you can't give the money to the person and tell him or her to pay the bill.

If your estate is approaching $600,000, which is the amount at which the federal estate tax kicks in, you may be able to use the gift exemption to push it below the taxable level, or at least to lower the taxable amount if your heirs will owe estate tax.

Insurance Benefits

If your life insurance is made payable to an individual, the proceeds are not probated. If your life insurance is made payable to your estate, the proceeds are probated. It's as simple as that. (For a complete discussion of life insurance see Chapter 4.)

Joint Property Ownership

Property you own jointly with another person does not pass through probate. Property owned by joint tenancy with right of survivorship automatically passes to your co-owner when you die. You can't leave it to anyone else, and your heir doesn't have to wait out the probate process. Property owned by tenancy by the entirety is very much like joint tenancy with right of survivorship, only the co-owners must be a married couple.

With both of these types of ownership you must have your spouse's consent to dispose of your property. If one spouse dies, the surviving spouse automatically inherits—no fuss, no hassle, no probate. These arrangements require written documentation specifying the type of ownership; for example, both names need to appear on the title to an automobile or a boat, or both names on the deed to a house or piece of real estate.

Another form of ownership, tenancy in common, doesn't bypass the probate process but you may decide in your will who should inherit your share of the property. If you and your spouse own a house under this form of ownership, you basically own half a house. The property is held in common, and you have the right to sell or give away your share as you wish.

In addition to avoiding probate, jointly owned property provides another side benefit: in many states creditors can't seize jointly held property unless the surviving spouse also assumed liability.

Trusts

Trusts are legal entities—they actually function like corporations—that own the property you transfer to them. The trust must be assigned a federal employer identification number, and if the trust income exceeds $600 a year, the trust must file state and federal income tax. A trust is managed by a trustee but owned by its beneficiaries.

All trusts are not created equal. Some trusts are set up inside your will, others outside. Some offer tax benefits, others don't. Some are probated, others aren't. Setting up a trust can be as simple as adding a few paragraphs to your will, but you will probably need help to make sure the trust does exactly what you want it to do.

There are two major types of trusts—*testamentary trusts*, which are created by your will when you die and are funded by your estate, and *inter vivos,* or *living trusts*, which are set up while you are alive. If you establish a living trust, you can serve as the trustee (or you can appoint someone else), and when you die, the trust's assets are distributed directly to your beneficiaries. It can be very easy to set up a living trust, but poorly executed trusts can become a legal nightmare and a costly mess for your heirs.

Some trusts are irrevocable—you can't make any changes once they are in place; others are revocable—you can modify the terms as you see fit. Each type of trust has its own strengths, weaknesses, and tax consequences. (See box below.)

A PRIMER ON TRUSTS

There are a number of different types of trusts to meet different needs. Here's a rundown of a few of the basic types:

Minor's Testamentary Trust. This trust is created by your will for the sole purpose of protecting your children's inheritance. Basically a trustee is appointed by you in your will to manage the assets for the children's benefit, preventing the guardian from mismanaging the funds. In addition a minor's testamentary trust can establish rules on when your children can get their hands on the money. The assets included in this type of trust do pass through probate.

Irrevocable 2503(c) Trust. This type of trust, named for the section of the Internal Revenue Code that governs it, may provide tax benefits. When you set up an irrevocable 2503(c) trust, you must surrender benefit from and control of the property held in the trust. You give up the power to control the trust property, and in exchange the trust's assets are no longer a part of your taxable estate. This type of trust is not established in your will; it is set up during your lifetime. It can be used for a child or an adult.

Living Trust. As the name implies, a living trust is one that you set up and transfer your assets into while you're alive. An immediate advantage to such a trust: You can avoid probate. You can also specify the exact conditions under which your assets will be distributed.

You can deposit your life insurance and death benefits from an employee-benefit plan into a living trust. Since a living trust isn't a part of your will, it isn't probated, and the contents don't become part of the public record, protecting your family's financial privacy.

Living trusts can be either irrevocable or revocable. A revocable living trust does not provide any estate tax savings, but this may not matter if your estate is worth less than $600,000. If it is worth more than that amount, you may consider establishing an irrevocable trust, which avoids estate tax but removes control of your assets from you.

Qualified Terminable Interest Property (QTIP) Trust. This type of trust allows you, rather than your spouse, to decide who will ultimately inherit your estate. (A QTIP trust prevents your spouse, should he or she remarry, from allowing his or her new spouse to squander your hard-earned assets, leaving your children with nothing.) A QTIP trust provides a lifetime income to the surviving spouse, but when he or she dies, the principal in the trust passes on to whomever you choose, usually your children.

Irrevocable Life Insurance Trust. To avoid paying estate taxes on life insurance proceeds, you can place your life insurance policies in a life insurance trust. The downside: When you set up a life insurance trust, you must give up all ownership rights, including the right to borrow against the policies and to change the beneficiaries. Also, if you die within three years of setting up the trust, your insurance will be included in your taxable estate anyway. If your beneficiary happens to die before you do, then your alternate beneficiary will collect.

If you want to set up a trust, consult with an attorney or estate-planning specialist. Some of the books in the Resources section of this chapter can also provide a more comprehensive overview of the use of trusts in estate planning.

KEEPING IT LEGAL

Any citizen of the United States who is over age 18 and is of sound mind may write his or her own will. If you do decide to draft your will yourself, keep these tips in mind:

- Be precise but don't use legalistic language: your heirs might have to grapple with legal realities you don't intend.
- Express all fractions, ages, and dollar amounts in both words and numbers to avoid misunderstandings: five thousand dollars ($5,000).
- Number pages to indicate the sequence and the total number of pages. For example: page one of three.
- Sign or initial the corner of each page other than the signature page.
- Type the final draft.
- Make no insertions or corrections. If you change or correct a typewritten draft, it's usually best to retype the whole document.
- Sign your name just after the bottom line of your will, leaving no room to slip in an extra line or paragraph.
- Have the will signed in the presence of witnesses who aren't beneficiaries to the will. Note: If witnesses are beneficiaries, they lose their legacies, and in some states your entire will is invalidated. Most states require only two witnesses, but it's best to be safe, so have three.

  Witnesses should be adults, preferably people who know you well. It's a good idea to have witnesses who are younger than you, because they're more likely to be available if there is a question about your will after your death.

  Witnesses don't have to know the contents of the will, but they should realize that they are witnessing the signature of your will. Each of the witnesses must sign his or her name and address in the presence of the others. If a signature is illegible, the witness should print his or her name underneath.
- To avoid confusion, execute, or sign, date, and witness, only one copy of your will. It's all right to make extra copies of the will, but mark them as copies.

Another alternative is a holographic will, one written entirely by hand. Holographic wills are recognized in about 30 states, but it usually makes more sense to take time to type the will out and have it witnessed to avoid any possible confusion. A holographic will does not need to be witnessed, but it does need to be properly constructed and the handwriting must be verified at the time the will goes through probate.

DEATH AND TAXES

Settling an estate includes settling with the tax man. While some people assume that they won't owe any taxes because of the modest size of their estates, you may be sure that Uncle Sam wants to share in your inheritance. Here's a brief rundown of the federal and state taxes that may apply to your estate:

Federal Taxes

Income Tax. When you die, the federal government still wants to collect tax on the income collected during your final days. It's up to your executor to file an income tax return for the estate.

Estate Tax. The vast majority of Americans don't owe any estate tax because it is collected only on estates worth more than $600,000. Estates above that threshold get clobbered: the estate tax starts at 37 percent and climbs to a whopping 50 percent by $2.5 million.

One exception: You can pass an unlimited amount of money to a spouse without paying any estate taxes. The catch is that when your spouse dies, the government will collect unless your spouse has done some fast and fancy estate planning. Since you never know if your spouse will die with you or shortly after you, you shouldn't count on claiming the marital deduction to avoid estate taxes.

When calculating your gross estate to decide if you need to take special steps to lower your taxable estate, take a look at the way you've set up your life insurance policies. Proceeds from life insurance policies paid to your estate are included in your taxable estate for federal tax purposes; those paid to other individuals or parties are not. For details see Chapter 4.

Gift Tax. You can give away as much as $10,000 to any number of people each year without paying any federal gift taxes. Your spouse can give away another $10,000, for a total of $20,000.

Any gifts you give that exceed the $10,000/$20,000 annual gift exclusion are subject to gift tax. The gift tax is linked with the federal estate tax. As discussed, you get a $600,000 exemption from federal estate taxes. If you give any gifts subject to gift tax, that amount is subtracted from the $600,000 estate tax exemption. Basically you have a personal exemption worth $600,000, and you can use it when you are alive as forgiveness of gift taxes or when you are dead for forgiveness of estate taxes.

Generation-Skipping Transfer Tax. This tax, sometimes called the "grandparent's tax," is imposed when your grandchildren or great-grandchildren inherit wealth from you. Here's the thinking behind this tax: The IRS wants to impose a death tax on your assets when you die, and it wants to tax your children when they die. Now, if you leave assets directly to your grandchildren (or great-grandchildren), then the IRS misses out on an opportunity to tax those assets. If you skip a generation (your children's generation) by giving or leaving your assets to your grandchildren, the IRS wants to make up for that loss by imposing a "generation-skipping tax."

The good news is that each person can exempt up to $1 million from this tax (married couples can exempt up to a total of $2 million). If you have enough money that you need to worry about this tax, then you have enough money to consult a lawyer and estate planner to help develop a detailed estate plan so that you can avoid it.

State Taxes

For tax rates in your state contact the state department of revenue and taxation. See the Resources section on page 31.

Income Tax. If you live in a state that collects income tax, your state government will want its share of your final wages, too. Again the responsibility of filing the state tax return falls on the shoulders of your executor.

Estate Tax. Laws vary from state to state.

STATES WHERE YOU CAN USE
THE UNIFORM TRANSFERS TO MINORS ACT (UTMA)

State	Age the Child Can Claim the Cash
Alabama	21
Alaska	18 (can be extended up to 25)
Arizona	21
Arkansas	21 (can be lowered to 18)
California	18 (can be raised to 25)
Colorado	21
District of Columbia	18
Florida	21
Georgia	21
Hawaii	21
Idaho	21
Illinois	21
Indiana	21
Iowa	21
Kansas	21
Kentucky	18
Maine	18 (can be raised to 21)
Maryland	21
Massachusetts	21
Minnesota	21
Missouri	21
Montana	21
Nevada	18
New Hampshire	21
New Jersey	21 (can be lowered to 18)
New Mexico	21
North Carolina	21 (can be lowered to 18)
North Dakota	21
Ohio	21
Oklahoma	18
Oregon	21
Rhode Island	18
South Dakota	18
Utah	21
Virginia	18 (can be raised to 21)
Washington	21
West Virginia	21
Wisconsin	21
Wyoming	21

Inheritance Tax. Inheritance tax is a tax imposed on the person inheriting the property; in most cases it is withheld from the bequest before it is distributed. Inheritance tax rates vary from state to state and with the relationship of the beneficiary to the testator: the closer the relationship, the lower the tax. For example, a spouse's inheritance might be taxed at 1 or 2 percent of its value while an unrelated friend might have to pay as much as a 20 percent tax. Almost half the states impose an inheritance tax; this tax is in addition to a state estate tax.

Gift Tax. A handful of states also levy state gift taxes. For details on state gift taxes contact your state department of taxation.

"ONE DAY THIS WILL ALL BE YOURS"

Minor children can't legally own much property without adult supervision. In most states once a child's bank account balance swells past the $2,500 or $5,000 mark, an adult must be responsible for managing the assets.

You can use the Uniform Transfers to Minors Act (UTMA) to leave gifts to your children if you live in one of the 38 states that have adopted the act or in the District of Columbia. The UTMA allows you to make a gift to a minor by appointing a custodian in your will to supervise the gifts. The assets must pass to the child at an age specified by law (see the chart on page 17).

Another option is the creation of a children's trust. The main advantage: you get to decide how old your children should be before they can get control of the property or assets you leave them in your will.

A children's trust is a legal entity created in your will. As with other trusts you must appoint a trustee who will manage the trust for your children, and that person must file state and federal taxes for the trust. The trustee manages the trust property and can spend it only for the beneficiary's "health, support, maintenance, and education."

It makes sense to use a children's trust if you don't live in a state that has adopted the UTMA—and if you have a significant amount of money to leave to your children. In most cases your gift needs to be worth more than $25,000 to justify the costs of managing the trust. The trustee is entitled to "reasonable compensation" for the service of managing the trust.

WHO WILL MANAGE YOUR AFFAIRS WHEN YOU CAN'T?

At the same time that you execute your will, you should execute two other equally important documents: a durable power of attorney for your legal matters and a durable power of attorney for health care (sometimes called an advance medical directive). Most powers of attorney expire after a stated period or event, but the durable power of attorney lasts until it is revoked.

A durable power of attorney is a signed, dated, and witnessed paper naming another person (usually a spouse, child, or close friend) who can make financial or medical decisions for you if you cannot make them for yourself. This eliminates the need for your family to go to court to have a guardian (or conservator) appointed by a judge if you become ill or incapacitated. More important, by filling out a durable power of attorney, *you* decide who will make the decisions on your behalf.

You can appoint a power of attorney on a temporary basis or on a long-term basis. Some states allow you to sign a "springing" power of attorney: one that springs into effect when needed.

The two types of authority require two separate documents. You may or may not wish to name the same person in the documents, but you probably can save time by executing them both together. In most states the documents need only to be notarized rather than witnessed. Give the original copy to the person who will be acting on your behalf and provide a duplicate to your attorney.

It may be a good idea to give your agent extra powers, such as the power to make gifts or the power to refuse bequests under other people's wills, for estate-planning purposes and because of asset limitations in the Medicaid program. Be sure to select an alternate in case your agent dies or becomes incapacitated.

For additional information, refer to the following:

- "Medicare and Advance Directive," by the U.S. Department of Health and Human Services. Cost: Free. Contact: Consumer Information Center—3C; P.O. Box 100, Pueblo, CO 81002;
- The Power of Attorney Book, by Denis Clifford. Cost: $14.95, plus $4 shipping and handling. Contact: Nolo Press, 950 Parker Street, Berkeley, CA 94710; (800) 992-6656.

You should also think seriously about executing a "living will," stating your desires for any action in the event that you are irreversibly incapacitated and your family is faced with decisions about extraordinary artificial-life-support equipment. (See page 21.)

If you want to make a gift to your children while you are alive, you can use your state's Uniform Gifts to Minors Act (UGMA). Every state that hasn't adopted the UTMA has adopted the UGMA. The biggest difference between the two acts is that the UTMA is used for gifts in a will, and the UGMA is not. In many states the UGMA can't be used to give real estate.

It's easy to set up a UGMA account with most financial institutions: no complicated legal documents are required. You can appoint yourself (or another adult you select) to serve as a custodian to supervise the assets held for your child. The custodian controls the property or funds until the child reaches an age specified by state law, usually 18 or 21.

The downside to using a UGMA account: Your gifts are irrevocable; you can't get the money back once it's given. And the child has the right to take control of the money at age 18 or 21, depending on the laws of your state. So if you put money for college in a UGMA account and your child decides to buy a sports car and see the world instead, you're stuck with his or her decision.

ISSUES TO DISCUSS:
WHAT PARENTS SHOULD TALK ABOUT

- ❏ How should we divide our property?
- ❏ What are our specific bequests and gifts?
- ❏ Do we want to donate to any charities?
- ❏ Who should serve as the executor? Alternate?
- ❏ At what age do we want our children to control their inheritance?
- ❏ How do we want our assets distributed if our children don't survive us?
- ❏ Do we need to take additional steps to avoid paying taxes?
- ❏ Should we own our major assets, such as houses, cars, and bank accounts, as tenants in common? As joint tenants with right of survivorship? As tenants by the entirety?
- ❏ Do we need to change the beneficiaries on our life insurance policies, pensions, and other accounts or policies?

❏ Will stepchildren or children from another marriage be taken care of fairly?

❏ How often should we update our will?

QUESTIONS & ANSWERS

How do I provide for my final arrangements?

As difficult as it may be to contemplate such things, if you have preferences about your funeral plans and other final arrangements, you may want to write a letter spelling out your wishes. This letter is separate from your will, but it should be kept with your will or given to your executor. In the letter state your preferences for final arrangements and plans for any organ donations. You should also include your father's name and your mother's maiden name (which may be needed for the death certificate). In most cases your executor will honor your wishes, but be aware that the contents of your letter aren't legally binding.

What is a living will?

A living will is a document stating your desires about being kept alive by extraordinary artificial-life-support equipment. Living wills, which are recognized in all 50 states and the District of Columbia, eliminate the need for relatives to go to court to obtain legal rulings about the use of life-support systems. If you write a living will and then reconsider, don't fret: a living will can be revoked just as a last will can.

Your living will must be signed in the presence of two witnesses; usually there are no restrictions as to who may serve as witnesses. A copy should be kept with your medical records, and give copies to family members as well. Laws vary from state to state, but you can get information and a free copy of a living will for your state by contacting: Choice in Dying, 200 Varick Street, New York, NY 10014; (212) 366-5540.

Do I have to write my will over if a beneficiary dies?

No, but you should write a codicil. To update, all you need to do is add a line saying, "The gift of $10,000 that I left to my cousin

Jonathan is hereby revoked; that gift shall become part of my residuary estate." Each codicil must be witnessed.

What's the difference between inheritance taxes and estate taxes?

Who pays the bill. Inheritance taxes are taxes paid by your heirs to the state on their inheritance. The tax is based on their share of the inheritance and their relationship to you. Estate taxes are federal taxes imposed on estates with assets in excess of $600,000; estate taxes are paid by the estate before gifts are distributed.

My wife and I own a sailboat. My wife is a landlubber who would never set sail. Can I give the boat to my brother in my will?

It depends on where you live and who bought the boat. If you live in a community property state, you and your wife are considered equal owners of all personal property acquired during marriage, even if only your name is on the title. (Exceptions include property owned before the marriage, gifts, and property you have inherited.) You can't give away the boat because you can't give away your wife's share.

If you live in a common-law state, however, you and your wife separately own whatever you've independently purchased with your own money; if the deed or title is in your name, the boat would be considered yours—and yours to give away.

Community property states are Arizona, California, Idaho, Nevada, New Mexico, Texas, Washington, and Wisconsin. The District of Columbia and all other states are common-law states, with the exception of Louisiana, which uses a different system.

Do I have to provide for my children equally?

No, you may divide your children's inheritance any way you wish. If you die without a will, however, all of your children—minor and adult, biological and adopted, legitimate and illegitimate—have an equal claim on your estate in most states. (Most states also provide your unborn children a share of your estate.)

If you want to distribute your estate unequally—perhaps because you have a child with special needs or you have previously given one child a large gift or helped with the down payment on a house—you must do so in a will. It's best to list the reasons for unequal treatment of your children in your will. Children who are treated unequally or who are excluded from your will are a likely source of will contests.

What happens if both my spouse and I die together in an accident?

It depends on whether or not your will has a simultaneous death clause, which allows your property to pass directly to your surviving heirs. You can also require that a beneficiary survive you by a certain length of time—say, 30 or 45 days—in order to inherit. This can save double taxation and court costs if you and your spouse die together or a beneficiary dies shortly after you do.

What is a life insurance trust?

A way of avoiding taxes and probate. A life insurance trust is set up while you are alive. Your life insurance death benefit is paid to the trust, avoiding estate taxes and probate. If you think that your—or your spouse's—estate will be sufficiently large to be subject to estate taxes, consider transferring your life insurance policy into a life insurance trust. Contact an estate-planning professional for help.

If I sell property to my child, is it subject to gift tax?

Yes, if the sale price is less than the fair market price. In such cases the difference between the sale price and the actual value is considered a gift.

What is a self-proving will?

It's a way to save time and trouble when it's time to probate your will. When a will is presented to the court, the witnesses may be called to "prove," or verify, their signature. Most often a copy of the will (or just the part that they signed) is sent to the witnesses, along with an affidavit to sign and return to the court.

To shortcut this process, you can "self-prove" your will by having your witnesses sign a statement about the circumstances under which the will was signed at the time of the initial signing. This document is notarized and attached to your will. All but five states—Mississippi, Vermont, Washington, West Virginia, and Wisconsin—recognize self-proving certificates. A codicil can also be self-proved.

How do I revoke my will?

You can revoke it by writing a new one or simply by destroying it—by tearing, cutting, burning, or just writing "revoked" on the page. You don't need a witness for revocation.

How can I keep my heirs from contesting my will?

If you want to be bossy from the grave, include in your will an *in terrorem* clause, which states that anyone who challenges the will is automatically disinherited. Most states will enforce a clause like that, but some states say that a will challenge brought for good cause (say, the testator was mentally ill or subject to undue influence) will not trigger the *in terrorem* clause.

Can I get the court to rule that my will is valid before I die?

In some states, yes. About half the states will allow you to deposit your will with the probate court while you are alive. After your death the will is retrieved from probate court file. Four states—Arkansas, Indiana, North Dakota, and Ohio—allow you to petition the court to check over your will and see if it's valid.

I live in New York but have a vacation home in Connecticut. Where do I go through probate?

Your estate is probated twice, since real estate must be probated in the state in which it is located. The probate in Connecticut is called an ancillary administration.

What happens if there isn't enough money in my estate to cover my taxes?

In most states any debts, taxes, and expenses of the estate are first taken out of the estate's general fund, or "residue." When the residue is gone, general bequests are reduced, then specific bequests are sold. It could be possible for your spouse and children to end up with less money than you or they expected because their funds in the residuary estate are depleted paying the estate taxes associated with property given to other heirs. To avoid this problem, plan your estate to minimize your tax liability and minimize your bequests outside the family.

Will my stepchildren inherit if I die without a will?

In most states stepchildren, as well as adopted children, children from a prior marriage, and illegitimate children, all inherit, unless you stipulate otherwise in your will.

Is my will still valid when I move to another state?

Moving from one state to another should have no effect on the validity of your will, provided it was valid at the time it was made. Since many laws vary from state to state, it's a good idea to have your will reviewed by a local attorney after you settle into your new home. And remember, real estate must be probated in the state in which it's located, so if you own property in more than one state, your will must go through probate more than once.

If I get a divorce, do I have to change the beneficiaries on all my insurance policies and bank accounts?

Definitely. If you divorce, your ex-spouse cannot inherit under your will in most states (in some states divorce invalidates the entire will). But divorce doesn't have any bearing on other beneficiary designations. For example, if your ex-spouse is named as beneficiary of a life insurance policy or an individual retirement account or other policy with an appointed beneficiary, your ex will collect when you die. If you don't want your ex-spouse to cash in, you must change the designations on the policies or accounts.

What do per stirpes and per capita mean?

Per stirpes and per capita are legal terms involving the distribution of your assets in your will to your grandchildren. Per stirpes literally means "by the root"; per capita means "by the head." If you distribute your estate per capita, every descendant receives an equal amount; if you distribute per stirpes, the estate is divided along the branches of your family tree. For example, let's say you have two children, Rodger and Shari. Rodger has three children and Shari has one. If you were to distribute your assets to your grandchildren per capita, each child would receive one-fourth of your estate. If you were to distribute per stirpes, Shari's child would receive half your estate and Rodger's children would each receive one-sixth.

If I videotape myself reading my will, is it legally valid?

No. A video could complement a typewritten will, but it can't take its place.

Where should I keep my will?

Give the original copy of your will to your attorney and keep a copy in your safe-deposit box. If appropriate, give a copy to the person you have named to serve as executor. (For more information on record keeping, see the appendix.)

STEP BY STEP:
WILL-AND ESTATE-PLANNING CHECKLIST

❑ Estimate your net worth (see page 27).
❑ Estimate your federal and state taxes.
❑ Assess your need for trusts and other estate-planning options to avoid taxes, if necessary.
❑ Consider any special needs of your heirs.
❑ Decide on the distribution of your assets.
❑ Select an executor and an alternate.
❑ Select a guardian and an alternate (see Chapter 2).
❑ Prepare a letter of final instruction.
❑ Establish a durable power of attorney.
❑ Write a living will.
❑ Draft and execute your will.
❑ Inform your family of your plans and wishes.
❑ Store your will in a secure location (see Chapter 10).

HOW MUCH ARE YOU WORTH?

Before you write your will, it helps to know how much you own. This is the first step in estate planning—and avoiding unnecessary taxes. You'll probably be surprised to find your estate worth more than you thought.

MY NET-WORTH STATEMENT

Name: _____   Date: _____

ASSETS

Assets Included in Your Will

Cash on hand _____

Individual checking account _____

Individual savings account _____

Certificates of deposit _____

Government securities _____

Mutual funds _____

Bonds _____

Stocks _____

IOUs _____

Life insurance to the estate _____

Share of business _____

Automobiles _____

Household furnishings _____

Art and antiques _____

Jewelry and furs _____

Other valuables _____

TOTAL: _____

Assets Usually Passed on Outside Your Will

Joint checking account
_____

Joint savings account
_____

Jointly owned property
_____

Trusts
_____

Life insurance to a specific beneficiary
_____

Individual retirement accounts
_____

Pension or retirement benefits
_____

TOTAL:
_____

LIABILITIES

Mortgage balance
_____

Loan balance
_____

Charge account balances
_____

Credit card balances
_____

Miscellaneous bills
_____

Taxes owed
_____

TOTAL:
_____

Total assets included in your will
_____

    PLUS   +
_____

Total assets passed outside your will
_____

    LESS   -
_____

Total liabilities
_____

    EQUALS   =
_____

NET WORTH:
_____

STATE BY STATE

Name of State	Court with Jurisdiction	Holographic Wills Recognized?	Self-Proving Wills Recognized?
Alabama	Probate court	Yes	Yes
Alaska	Superior court	Yes	Yes
Arizona	Superior court	Yes	Yes
Arkansas	Probate court	Yes	Yes
California	Superior court	Yes	Yes
Colorado	District court*	Yes	Yes
Connecticut	Probate court	No	Yes
Delaware	Court of chancery	No	Yes
District of Columbia	Superior court	No	Yes
Florida	Circuit court	No	Yes
Georgia	Probate court	No	Yes
Hawaii	Circuit court	No	Yes
Idaho	District court	Yes	Yes
Illinois	Circuit court	No	No
Indiana	Circuit or superior court*	No	Yes
Iowa	District court	Yes	Yes
Kansas	District court	No	Yes
Kentucky	District court	Yes	Yes
Louisiana	District court	Yes	Yes
Maine	Probate court	Yes	Yes
Maryland	Orphan's court*	Military only	Yes
Massachusetts	Probate and family court	No	Yes
Michigan	Probate court	Yes	Yes
Minnesota	Probate court	No	Yes
Mississippi	Chancery court	Yes	Yes
Missouri	Circuit court	No	Yes
Montana	District court	Yes	Yes
Nebraska	County court	Yes	Yes
Nevada	District court	Yes	Yes
New Hampshire	Probate court	No	Yes
New Jersey	Surrogate's court	Yes	Yes
New Mexico	Probate or district	No	Yes
New York	Surrogate's court	Military only	Yes
North Carolina	Superior court	Yes	Yes
North Dakota	County court	Yes	Yes
Ohio	Court of common pleas	No	Yes
Oklahoma	District court	Yes	Yes
Oregon	Circuit or county court	No	Yes
Pennsylvania	Common pleas court	Yes	Yes
Rhode Island	Probate court	Yes	Yes

Name of State	Court with Jurisdiction	Holographic Wills Recognized?	Self-Proving Wills Recognized?
South Carolina	Probate court	No	Yes
South Dakota	Circuit court	Yes	Yes
Tennessee	Chancery court*	Yes	Yes
Texas	County or probate	Yes	Yes
Utah	District court	Yes	Yes
Vermont	Probate court	No	No
Virginia	Circuit court	Yes	Yes
Washington	Superior court	No	Yes
West Virginia	County commissioner	Yes	No
Wisconsin	Circuit court	No	No
Wyoming	District court	No	Yes

*May vary from county to county within the state.

YOUR GIFT LIST

SPECIFIC GIFTS

Item	Recipient
Antiques, automobiles, books, clothing, collectibles, furs, heirlooms, jewelry, silver, etc	

_____

_____

_____

_____

_____

_____

_____

_____

_____

_____

_____

_____

GENERAL GIFTS

Amount	Recipient
$	
$	
$	

CHARITABLE GIFTS

Amount	Organization
$	
$	
$	

RESOURCES:
WHERE TO GO FOR MORE INFORMATION

BOOKS

■ **The Complete Will Kit**, by Jens C. Appel III and F. Bruce Gentry. Cost: $19.95. Contact: John Wiley & Sons, 1 Wiley Drive, Somerset, NJ 08875; (800) 225-5945.

■ **How to Use Trusts to Avoid Probate and Taxes: A Guide to Living, Marital, Support, Charitable, and Insurance Trusts**, by Theresa Meehan Rudy, Kay Ostberg, and Jean Dimeo, in association with HALT. Cost: $10, plus $1.50 shipping and handling. Contact: HALT Membership Services Department, 1319 F Street NW, Suite 300, Washington, DC 20004; (202) 347-9600.

■ **Keys to Preparing a Will**, by James John Jurinski, J.D., CPA. Cost: $5.95, plus $1.75 shipping and handling. Contact: Barron's Educational Series, 250 Wireless Blvd., Hauppauge, NY 11788; (800) 645-3476.

■ **Nolo's Simple Will Book**, by Denis Clifford. Cost: $17.95, plus $4 shipping and handling. Good in all states except Louisiana. Contact: Nolo Press, 950 Parker Street, Berkeley, CA 94710; (800) 992-6656.

■ **Make Your Own Living Trust**, by Denis Clifford. Cost: $19.95, plus $4 shipping and handling. Contact: Nolo Press, 950 Parker Street, Berkeley, CA 94710; (800) 992-6656.

■ **A Parent's Guide to Wills and Trusts**, by Don Silver. Cost: $11.95, plus $3 shipping and handling. Contact: Adams-Hall Publishing, P.O. Box 491002-WC, Los Angeles, CA 90049; (800) 888-4452.

■ **Wills: A Do-It-Yourself Guide**, by HALT: An Organization of Americans for Legal Reform. Cost: $8.95, plus $1.50 shipping and handling. Contact: HALT Membership Services Department, 1319 F Street NW, Suite 300, Washington, DC 20004; (202) 347-9600.

COMPUTER SOFTWARE

■ **WillMaker**, Nolo Press/Legisoft. Software, plus a 200-page legal manual. Good in all states except Louisiana. Cost: $69.95. Contact: Nolo Press, 950 Parker Street, Berkeley, CA 94710; (800) 992-6656.

BROCHURES

■ The following free publications are available from the Internal Revenue Service:
"Federal Estate and Gift Taxes" (Publication 448);
"Survivors, Executors and Administrators" (Publication 559).
To receive a copy, call the IRS at (800) 829-3676.

■ For a free copy of the government brochure "Medicare and Advance Directives" write Consumer Information Center—3B, P.O. Box 100, Pueblo, CO 81002.

ORGANIZATIONS

• **HALT: Help Abolish Legal Tyranny, An Organization of Americans for Legal Reform**, 1319 F Street NW, Suite 300, Washington, DC 20004-1150; (202) 347-9600.

- **American Bar Association**, 750 North Lake Shore Drive, Chicago, IL 60611; (312) 988-5000.

STATE DEPARTMENTS OF REVENUE AND TAXATION

Alabama, (205) 242-1000
Alaska, (907) 465-2370
Arizona, (602) 255-3381
Arkansas, (501) 682-7250
California, (800) 852-5711
Colorado, (303) 534-1208
Connecticut, (203) 566-7033
Delaware, (302) 577-3300
District of Columbia, (202) 727-6103
Florida, (904) 488-6800
Georgia, (404) 656-4071
Hawaii, (808) 587-4242
Idaho, (208) 334-7660
Illinois, (217) 782-3336
Indiana, (317) 232-2240
Iowa, (515) 281-3114
Kansas, (913) 296-3051
Kentucky, (502) 564-4580
Louisiana, (504) 925-4611
Maine, (207) 287-2076
Maryland, (410) 225-1995
Massachusetts, (617) 727-4545
Michigan, (800) 487-7000
Minnesota, (612) 296-3781
Mississippi, (601) 359-1141
Missouri, (314) 751-3505

Montana, (406) 444-2837
Nebraska, (402) 471-5729
Nevada, (702) 687-4820
New Hampshire, (603) 271-2191
New Jersey, (609) 588-3800
New Mexico, (505) 827-0700
New York, (518) 438-6777
North Carolina, (919) 733-4682
North Dakota, (701) 224-3450
Ohio, (614) 846-6712
Oklahoma, (405) 521-4321
Oregon, (503) 378-4988
Pennsylvania, (717) 787-8201
Rhode Island, (401) 277-2905
South Carolina, (803) 737-4709
South Dakota, (605) 773-3311
Tennessee, (615) 741-3581
Texas, (512) 463-4400
Utah, (801) 530-4848
Vermont, (802) 828-2865
Virginia, (804) 367-8031
Washington, (800) 647-7706
West Virginia, (304) 558-3333
Wisconsin, (608) 266-2486
Wyoming, (307) 754-2686

GLOSSARY: UNDERSTANDING THE TERMS

Administrator: A person or an institution appointed by the court to manage the probate of the estate of a person who has died without a valid will.

Ancillary administration: The probate process in a second state that takes place when real estate is located in a state other than the one where the deceased lived. Because a probate court has jurisdiction in only its own state, when the deceased owns property in another state, an additional ancillary administration must be conducted there.

Annual exclusion: The amount that can be given by one person to another in a calendar year without the giver's incurring federal gift tax liability. Currently the limit is $10,000 per year.

Beneficiary: A person, organization, or institution named in a will to receive part of an estate. Also, someone who receives payment from an insurance policy or income from a trust.

Codicil: An amendment to an original will that adds to, deletes from, or otherwise changes the provisions of the will; executed and witnessed in the same manner as the original will.

Death tax: Another name for inheritance tax or estate tax.

Durable power of attorney: A legal document authorizing someone to make financial or medical decisions on your behalf if you become ill or incapacitated.

Elective share: The right of a surviving spouse to choose to receive dower or courtesy rights; a share (usually half) of the new estate rather than the amount specified in the will.

Escheat: The taking of estate property by the state when there are no surviving beneficiaries or heirs to receive it.

Executor: A person named by the testators in a will to administer the estate.

Executrix: A female executor.

Holographic will: A will written entirely by hand by the testator.

Intestate: Dying without a will.

Irrevocable: A trust that cannot be changed, amended, revoked, or canceled after it is created.

Probate: The process of proving the validity of a will in the appropriate court.

Surety bond: A type of insurance that protects your estate and beneficiaries if the executor mismanages or steals your assets.

Testator: The person making the will.

CHAPTER 2

YOUR ANGEL'S GUARDIAN

Picking the Best Guardian for Your Child

NUTS AND BOLTS

Most parents wouldn't dream of going out for the evening without arranging for a baby-sitter and leaving a detailed list of emergency phone numbers. But many of these same parents have not taken steps to arrange for a legal guardian to take care of their children if something serious should happen to them.

Granted, it's difficult to think about naming a guardian. It's heart-wrenching to imagine not being there to watch your kids grow up, but working out a contingency plan is part of being a responsible parent. Not naming a guardian can cause your children considerable trauma, as well as the possible expense and hassle of legal challenges. And if you are divorced, remarried, or living with an unmarried partner, the possibilities for conflict and confusion are almost infinite.

If you die without a will naming a guardian, the court will choose one for you. Unless you make your wishes known, there is no guarantee that the judge will appoint the person you think would provide the best care and support for your child. As a parent, selecting a guardian is one of the most important parts of your will. Doesn't your child deserve the security of having you appoint the best guardian possible?

TYPES OF GUARDIANSHIP

At the most basic level, a guardian is an adult who is legally responsible for a child. Ideally the guardian will serve as a surrogate parent who will lovingly guide your child into adulthood just as you would have done.

There are two main types of guardianship—the guardian of the person and the guardian of the property, also called guardian of the estate. A single person can be appointed to serve both roles or the responsibilities can be divided into two separate guardianships.

The guardian of the person is the adult responsible for the day-to-day care of your child. This is the person who signs the permission slips for school trips and bakes brownies for the class Halloween party. The guardian of the person will raise your child, so it's absolutely critical that you select the right person. It may also be helpful to provide for the guardian a letter describing your views on parenting and outlining instructions on how you want your children raised. The views expressed in the letter won't be legally binding, but instructions may help your guardian fulfill your wishes. The checklist on page 44 can provide some assistance in drafting a letter of parental guidance.

The guardian of the person has legal custody of the child—and the legal duty to take care of him or her. Personal guardians have the same basic rights as parents to consent to and request medical treatment for the child, including the right to add the child to a health insurance plan if the insurance company allows. Personal guardians can apply for Social Security benefits on the child's behalf (if the child's parents worked and paid Social Security taxes), register the child for school, and sign all the parental waiver forms marked "Signed by parent or guardian."

What the guardian of the person can't do is spend the child's money. The guardian of the person can handle relatively small financial matters on the child's behalf, often no more than $300 a month.

The guardian of the property, also called a conservator in some states, controls the purse strings. This guardian oversees and manages the child's financial assets until age 18 or 21, depending on the state.

To protect the child's assets, state law prohibits children from owning much property without supervision. Most states require a guardian of the property if the inheritance exceeds $5,000, if the child is the beneficiary of a life insurance policy, or if the court decides that a property guardian would be beneficial for the child.

When selecting a guardian of the property, look for someone who knows how to balance a checkbook, but not necessarily someone who is a "Wall Street Week" devotee. The guardian must be able to keep track of money, but extensive financial expertise isn't necessary.

State laws require that the guardian of the property use the money and other assets for the support, maintenance, and education of the child. To protect the child's inheritance, the court watches over the guardian's shoulder by requiring a periodic accounting to the court. The specific rules and timetables for the accounting vary from state to state.

The property guardian is required to manage the minor's assets prudently: speculative investing in too-good-to-be-true real estate deals or telemarketing schemes isn't allowed. The guardian can't combine funds with the minor or borrow any money from the child's account for personal use even if the guardian intends to pay it back. In most states the guardian must account for how every penny is spent and must get permission to spend principal.

In many cases a single person serves as both guardian of the person and guardian of the property. The most common reason for separating guardianship responsibility is that the person whom you trust to take care of your child may not be well suited to manage the money that will be left to the child, especially if your child will receive a large inheritance.

A WORD ABOUT PROCESS

Guardians—both personal and property—are appointed by the court. If something happened to you and your spouse, the person or persons named in your will to serve as guardians would go to the clerk of the court in the county where your children live to obtain and file the necessary paperwork to become guardians. The paperwork shouldn't be too burdensome, and officers of the court should be able to provide assistance.

Most guardianships are not contested, but the law requires that certain immediate relatives of the child be notified in advance about the guardianship proceedings. If there are going to be fireworks over your selection of guardians, this is the stage when the sparks start to fly. You can go a long way toward smoothing over this process by talking with your relatives about your decision at the time you select your guardians.

Guardians of the property must often post bond, usually at the same rate as the executor's bond, 1 percent of the value of the estate being managed. In your will you can waive the bond, though some states require a guardian's bond even when it's waived in the will.

Once appointed, a guardian serves until released by the court from the duties. Guardianships are usually terminated when the child reaches age 18, when the guardian formally resigns due to ill health or trouble controlling the child, or when the court determines that the appointed guardian is no longer appropriate. The court will end a guardianship if the guardian is convicted of a felony, abuses the child, or otherwise fails to take adequate care of the child.

SELECTING THE RIGHT GUARDIAN

Naming the right guardian is too important a decision to leave to someone you don't know. Even with the best of intentions, a judge who does not know you or your other family members may not be able to make the best choice. It can be very difficult to name a guardian, especially if more than one person wants to serve. Though it's easier said than done, don't feel obligated to name a particular relative or friend as a test of loyalty or trust. The decision is far too important to allow family politics to dictate your choice. Do what is best for your child.

Discuss with your partner your selection of a guardian. Keep in mind that although it is possible to name joint guardians, there are fewer chances of complications if you name just one. You don't want your child to be caught in a custody battle if you name a couple that later divorces.

The box on page 39 can help you pick the most appropriate candi-

ISSUES TO CONSIDER
WHEN PICKING A GUARDIAN

- How old is the person?
- Is the person in good physical health?
- Is the person loving? Kind? Happy?
- Does your child enjoy spending time with the person?
- Does the person have a stable marriage or relationship?
- Does the person have other children? If so, does your child enjoy spending time with those children?
- Does the person's family tend to get along? Do they enjoy each other?
- Does the person have the time and energy to devote to raising your child?
- Can the person handle the ongoing responsibility of serving as a legal guardian?
- Is the person a good role model? Does the person smoke? Drink too much? Use excessive profanity?
- Does the person live in a community where you would want your child to grow up?
- Would there be problems with other relatives over the selection of the person?
- Can the person manage your child's assets and handle filing the necessary reports with the court?
- Does the person have the financial resources to help support your child if necessary?
- Does the person share your religious and moral beliefs?
- Does the person share your ideas about education?
- Does the person agree with your attitudes about child rearing and

date. You and your partner should both write a will and appoint the same person so that there will be no confusion if you should die together. You should also appoint one or two backups in case your first choice can't serve, won't serve, or decides to resign from the job after a few years.

If you feel strongly that a certain relative should not be named guardian, you can also specify in your will the names of people you do not want to serve. For example, if you are in a second marriage and have custody of your children, you may want the children's stepparent to serve as guardian rather than letting custody fall to the bio-logical parent. Of course, you can't prevent your former spouse from contesting or challenging your designated guardian in court, but when considering the case, the judge will take note of your objections. Remember, though, your will is not a place to vent your hostilities about the failures of your first marriage; in fact, you should be very careful about how you word such a passage in your will. When your will is probated, it becomes a public document, and derogatory remarks about potential guardians could be grounds for a libel lawsuit against your estate. If you want to exclude someone as guardian, con-sider consulting a lawyer for the exact language to use in your will.

Under most state laws the biological parent has paramount right to custody of the children. (The rules of surrogacy vary from state to state: for more information contact the Center for Surrogate Parenting; see the Resources section.) But in a custody dispute—even one between a guardian candidate and a natural parent—the judge will take a number of factors into consideration, including the length of the marriage (or relationship), how involved the biological parent was in the child's life, and the wishes of the children. The stepparent or other guardian nominee can increase the likelihood of being named if he or she has legally adopted the child or made the child a beneficiary of his or her will. In such cases the stated wishes of the deceased natural parent can play a critical role in the decision-making process.

Once you and your spouse have decided whom to ask to be a guardian, pick a quiet time to discuss the issue with the person. While it is an honor to be asked to be a guardian—what greater measure of trust is there?—it is also a tremendous responsibility. Use the ques-tions on page 44 as a guide when discussing the issue with your poten-tial guardians. Do not ask the person to respond at once. In fact, urge the person to consider it at length and to get back to you at some later time.

If they are old enough to understand what you are talking about, be sure to talk to your kids and ask them about their wishes. Let your kids know that they have nothing to be afraid of, that you are simply making sure that they will always be taken care of.

ISSUES TO DISCUSS:
WHAT PARENTS SHOULD TALK ABOUT

- ❏ Whom should we consider as guardians?
- ❏ Whom should we consider as alternates?
- ❏ How will our choice affect other family members?
- ❏ Do we need a separate guardian for the person and guardian for the property?
- ❏ If we have more than one child, do we want to make sure the children stay together?
- ❏ Do we want our children to be adopted by the guardian?
- ❏ Do any of our children have special needs that require particular skills or patience in a guardian?
- ❏ How often will we review our choices to make sure that they are still the best for our children?
- ❏ How do we want our children raised if we're not here?

QUESTIONS & ANSWERS

What is the difference between adoption and guardianship?

Adoption is forever. For all purposes and for all time, the adopting adult becomes the legal parent of the child. With a guardianship the legal relationship ends when the child reaches age 18. If a biological parent puts his or her child up for adoption, the parent forfeits all parental rights and obligations to the child. If a biological parent surrenders responsibility of a child to a legal guardian, the parent still has a legal relationship with the child.

What happens if two people want guardianship of the same child?

A judge must decide who should be appointed guardian. Usually courts follow a system of preference when selecting a guardian. First they usually give custody to the natural parent, if living. Next they usually choose the person with whom the child has been living in a "wholesome and stable" environment. Next they usually choose a person deemed suitable and able to provide adequate and proper care and guidance for the child. After weighing the facts, the judge has the final word.

Does the child have any voice in selecting the guardian?

It depends on where you live and the age of your child. If a child is over 14 years of age (12 in some states), the child has some power in naming the guardian. In some states if the minor child selects a qualified person to serve, the court must appoint that person. Other states simply agree to consider the child's choice when making the decision.

Can a guardianship be established informally with a letter of agreement between a parent and another adult?

No. A court-ordered legal guardianship requires that the guardian file legal documents in court, appear before a judge in a hearing, and be appointed guardian.

Do all children need guardians?

No. Children under 18 don't need guardians if they have achieved legal adult status, usually by marriage, military service, or court order. In some cases a guardian of the estate can be appointed for the financial assets of such a minor.

I know I can't prevent my ex-husband from getting custody of my children after my death, but can I prevent him from getting control of their money?

You can name another guardian in your will and hope that the judge respects your wishes. But as you point out, the children's biological father will probably receive custody unless he is unfit to serve. While the court may appoint your ex-husband guardian of the person, you can name a separate guardian for your children's assets.

My children will inherit a considerable amount of money when I die. The family I would like them to be raised with has a more modest lifestyle. How can I protect my children from resentment from the guardian's other children?

You are wise to be concerned about possible resentment. Consider sharing the wealth. You might want to consider making provisions for the guardian of the property to provide funds to the family to build an addition onto their home if additional space is required or to help finance the college education of the guardian's other children. Be careful about establishing such an arrangement. You want to make sure that if your financial situation changes between the time you write your will and the time a guardian is appointed, your children will still be properly taken care of.

I have two children, one from a previous marriage. Do they have to have the same guardian?

Not necessarily. The court tries to name a guardian in the "best interests of the child." While many judges do try to keep families together as much as possible, brothers and sisters are not required by law to stay together.

STEP BY STEP: NAMING A GUARDIAN

- ❑ Decide whether you need a separate guardian for the person and guardian for the property.
- ❑ Discuss with your partner whom you would like to serve as guardian(s).
- ❑ Select one or two alternates for each guardianship.
- ❑ Write a letter of parental guidance outlining your wishes about how you would like your children to be raised (see checklist).
- ❑ Ask the guardian if he or she would be willing to serve.
- ❑ Discuss your letter of parental guidance and ask if there would be any problems with following your wishes.
- ❑ Ask the alternates if they would be willing to serve.
- ❑ If your children are old enough, discuss your selections of guardians with them. Listen to any reasons your children have for not feeling comfortable with your choice.
- ❑ Name the guardians in your will.
- ❑ Keep your will current. If you have additional children or if the status of one of your guardians changes due to birth, death, marriage, divorce, or some other major change, ask whether he or she is still willing to serve.

QUESTIONS TO ASK A PROSPECTIVE GUARDIAN

- ❑ Do you feel capable of providing my children with all the emotional support and love that may be required?
- ❑ Do you have the time and energy to raise my child?
- ❑ How many children of your own do you want?
- ❑ Would you anticipate problems or conflicts with your children if you were to become a guardian?
- ❑ In what ways would you treat my children differently than you treat your own?
- ❑ Do you agree with my ideas about child rearing?
- ❑ What kind of religious or moral training would you provide for my child?
- ❑ Would you be willing to raise all of my children? Even if you have more at a later date?
- ❑ Would you provide financial support for my children if their inheritance is insufficient to cover all their needs?
- ❑ Would you be willing to serve as guardian until my youngest child reaches age 18?
- ❑ What kind of relationship do you think you will have with my children after the guardianship has ended?
- ❑ Would you be sure that my child visits with relatives on both sides of the family?

ISSUES TO COVER IN A LETTER OF PARENTAL GUIDANCE

A letter of parental guidance can help a guardian understand the way you would like your child to be raised. Let these questions stimulate your thinking, but don't be too rigid. Keep in mind that times change: what seems appropriate today may seem hopelessly out-of-date 10 years from now. You don't want your guardian to feel restricted or your children to feel guilty because you have created an unrealistic code of behavior.

- ❑ Allowance: How much? Does your child have to do any chores to collect it? At what age should it start? Stop?
- ❑ Discipline: What methods do you approve of? What methods do you want to avoid?

❏ Education: Do you want your child to attend public, private, or parochial schools? Do you want your child to take music lessons? What are your attitudes about after-school sports and activities? What kind of focus do you want on college and professional training?

❏ Religion: What kind of religious training do you want your children to have? Which rituals are important to you?

❏ Holidays and traditions: What family practices do you want to continue?

❏ Dating: At what age can your child begin dating? Going out in groups? Curfews?

❏ After-school work: At what age can your child begin to work? Any restrictions on hours? Jobs?

❏ Summer jobs: Do you want your child to work in summers? Any restrictions? Should part of the money go toward college?

❏ Driving: How old do you want your child to be before getting a driver's license? Any restrictions?

❏ Buying a car: Would you allow your child to purchase a car? A motorcycle?

❏ Family medical history: What health problems might your child be susceptible to?

❏ Family secrets: When (if ever) do you want your children to learn about the skeletons in the family closet? Do you want them to be told, or do they have to ask?

RESOURCES: WHERE TO GO FOR MORE INFORMATION

BOOKS

■ **The Guardianship Book**, by Lisa Goldoftas and Attorney David Brown. Cost: $19.95, plus $4 shipping and handling. Contact: Nolo Press, 950 Parker Street, Berkeley, CA 94710; (800) 992-6656. (The book discusses instructions and forms to obtain a legal guardianship in California; specific laws and procedures will vary in other states.)

■ **A Legal Guide for Lesbian and Gay Couples**, by Hayden Curry and Denis Clifford. Cost: $17.95, plus $4 shipping and handling. Contact: Nolo Press, 950 Parker Street, Berkeley, CA 94710; (800) 992-6656.

■ Guardianships are discussed in many books on writing wills.

ORGANIZATIONS OF INTEREST

• **Guardian Association**, P.O. Box 6231, Clearwater, FL 34618; (813) 448-0730.

• **Center for Surrogate Parenting**, 8383 Wilshire Blvd., Suite 750, Beverly Hills, CA 90211; (213) 655-1974.

GLOSSARY: UNDERSTANDING THE TERMS

Adopt: To take a child legally into one's family to raise as one's own child; to accept all the legal rights and responsibilities of a natural parent.

Contest: To object, either in person or in writing, to a legal proceeding, in this case to the appointment of a guardian.

Legal custody: The court-ordered right to have legal authority or control of a minor child.

Guardian of the person: An individual appointed by a court to be responsible for meeting a minor child's physical, medical, educational, emotional, and health needs; a child's legal custodian.

Guardian of the property: An individual appointed by a court to be responsible for managing and overseeing a minor child's assets and property.

CHAPTER 3

BEYOND THE ID BRACELET

Your Child's Legal Identity

NUTS AND BOLTS

Your child has a legal identity—as well as legal rights—from the moment he or she is born. In the days and weeks after your baby's birth, you will have to file some paperwork to formalize your baby's legal identity.

First you must select a name, then you will have to fill out and sign a birth certificate and request a Social Security number. And to ensure that your child will be covered under your health insurance policy, someone should notify your insurance company as soon as your child is born.

OBTAINING A BIRTH CERTIFICATE

If your baby is born in a hospital or birthing center, someone on staff will take care of the paperwork in processing the birth certificate. Shortly after your baby is born, a nurse or registrar will ask you for the baby's name and for other information necessary to complete the birth certificate. Some parents who have trouble settling on a name refer to this staffer as a member of the Name Police. This person will type up the form and present it to the parents and the doctor to sign before sending it to the state's vital statistics division to be recorded permanently.

Carefully check every word on the certificate before signing it. It's much easier to avoid mistakes than to correct them. Once the birth information is recorded by the state, you can request copies of the birth certificate, which are needed for passports, some jobs, and legal transactions.

In the unlikely event that your baby is born on the way to the hospital, the hospital attendant will still help you take care of filling out the forms. If you plan on having a home birth, you may need to get the birth certificate forms on your own. To obtain a copy of an application for a birth certificate, contact your state bureau of vital records. A complete listing of the offices is in the Resources section of the appendix.

The birth certificate includes a listing of the vital statistics about you and your baby, including the parents' names, place and date of birth, and the baby's exact time of arrival, sex, weight, and length. Many application forms also include questions about other children, previous miscarriages or children's deaths, and the educational levels of both parents. This information is used by the state bureau of vital statistics, but it will not appear on the final birth certificate in most states.

If you adopt a child, the adoption decree works much like a birth certificate. As parents you and your partner will select the child's given names, including the family name. All the names are recorded in the decree. In most states a new birth certificate is drawn up, though the place of birth is usually left unchanged. The original birth certificate is usually sealed with the adoption papers, and the new certificate takes the place of the old one.

Laws vary from state to state regarding birth certificates for children born to surrogate mothers and children conceived through artificial insemination. Many state laws on surrogacy require that the biological woman be listed on the birth certificate as the mother but allow for the name to be changed when the woman who will raise the child legally adopts the infant. If a married woman conceives a child through artificial insemination, the husband's name is usually listed on the birth certificate; if a sperm donor is used, the requirements differ from state to state. For additional information contact the Center for Surrogate Parenting, listed in the Resources section.

CHANGING NAMES

With the stroke of a pen, Archibald Leach became Cary Grant, Diane Belmont turned into Lucille Ball, and Marion Morrisson took on the identity of John Wayne. Like these famous movie stars, every year more than 50,000 Americans go to court to legally change their names.

While most of the new names go to adults, sometimes parents legally change their children's names after a divorce or remarriage—or simply because the name they originally chose no longer seems suitable.

The laws regarding name changes vary from state to state. In some places a simple affidavit signed by the parents is all that's required to make a legal name change. In other places, however, parents must show proof of an established new name, such as a baptismal certificate, an insurance policy, an immunization record, or the family Bible record.

When a name change requires a court order, the parents must petition a county probate court, a superior court, or a district court, following state laws. In some cases you must publish a notice of the intended change in the newspaper. Once the procedure is complete, the court issues a change of name order or decree. Sometimes new birth certificates are issued; other times the original certificates are simply amended.

APPLYING FOR A SOCIAL SECURITY NUMBER

Though your baby is too young to have a job, no child is too young to have a Social Security number. If your child receives money or investments, you may need a Social Security number to open an account in your child's name. You may be able to save money in the long run by keeping your child's money in a separate account, since interest earned in your children's account will be taxed at your child's rate but interest earned in your accounts will be taxed at your rate, which is probably higher.

Even if your little one isn't ready to enter the world of high finance, you will be ready to enter your child as a tax deduction come April 15. The Internal Revenue Service now requires that each child who reaches age one in a given tax year have a Social Security number. For example, if your child is born in October 1993, you will have to list the child and his or her Social Security number on your 1994 tax return. The penalty for not listing a Social Security number for a child you claim as a deduction is a stiff $50. If you apply for a Social Security number but your child is not yet assigned one by the filing due date, write "applied for" on the tax return.

Getting a Social Security number for a baby is simple. Most states now participate in the "numeration of birth" program, so that you can obtain a Social Security card at the same time you get a birth certificate by simply asking that the state department of vital statistics share the information with the Social Security Administration. No extra forms, no hassles.

If you don't apply for the Social Security number when you register the birth with the state, you can either go to your local Social Security office (look under U.S. Government in the phone book) or call the Social Security Administration's toll-free number, (800) 772-1213, and request SS-5, Application for a Social Security Number.

You will have to provide documents that show your identity, such as a driver's license, employee ID card, passport, marriage or divorce records, health insurance card, or insurance policy. For a child, a doctor or hospital bill will be accepted. Six to eight weeks after filing the paperwork either in person or by mail, your baby will receive a Social Security card and number by mail.

If you adopt an older child who already has a Social Security number, all you need to do is register the change of name with the Social Security Administration either by contacting the local office or by calling (800) 772-1213.

Don't fall for any of the services that offer to help you get a Social Security card—for a fee. Many of these companies have lofty names using the words "federal" or "government." Don't be suckered. Applying for a Social Security card is easy and it's free.

NOTIFYING YOUR INSURANCE COMPANY OF YOUR CHILD'S BIRTH

As soon as your baby is born, be sure to notify your health insurance company. Every insurer has a slightly different procedure, so find out what you need to do *before* the stork arrives.

If you are adopting a child, check with your insurance company about health coverage before you get custody of the child. Some insurance companies won't cover the child until the adoption has been finalized, a period that may be anywhere from three months to two years. Others cover the baby at the time of placement but exclude any preexisting conditions. That can be a real problem since an estimated 15 percent of the children adopted each year in the United States have some kind of preexisting condition. The American Medical Association is calling on the health insurance industry to change its ways and treat adopted children the same as biological ones, but in the meantime check with your insurance company to find out if you're covered. For more information contact Adoptive Families of America, 3333 Highway 100-N, Minneapolis, MN 55422; (612) 535-4829.

ISSUES TO DISCUSS: WHAT PARENTS SHOULD TALK ABOUT

- ❑ What should we name the baby?
- ❑ Who will be responsible for double-checking the birth certificate information?
- ❑ Who will file the paperwork necessary for Social Security?
- ❑ Where will we keep the baby's birth certificate and Social Security card? Adoption papers, if necessary?
- ❑ Who will notify the health insurance company of the baby's birth?

QUESTIONS & ANSWERS

Are there any restrictions on my choice of first names?

Very few. Johnny Cash made famous "A Boy Named Sue," but a review of birth records show that Sue's Boy Scout troop might also have included boys named Angel and Lovie and Alice. Equally unfortunate are those boys named Magnum, Demon, Pitbull—or simply Male. Girls have fared no better: parents have named their girls Frank, Dave, and Joe, as well as the tough-to-live-up-to Beauty and Cutie and Dandy.

The only definitive no-no in the name game is the use of numbers. When a Minneapolis man went to court to legally change his name to the number 1069, the judge refused to allow it, arguing that replacing proper names with numerical digits would "hasten that day in which we all become lost in faceless numbers."

Can I choose my baby's surname?

It depends on where you live. In days gone by, custom dictated that a baby use the surname of his father if his parents were married or of his mother if they were not. But today many women do not take on their husband's names after marriage, so the issue has become more complex.

Some states require that if the parents are married, then the father's last name be used. In these states if the parents are not married, some require that the mother's last name must be used, and others allow the mother to pick a name. Most states allow parents to use hyphenated last names for their children, even when reciting the child's full name becomes a tongue twister.

If you're not sure whether the surname you have chosen for your child is legal in your state, check with the state department of vital records (see the Resources section of Chapter 10, "Setting Your Records Straight").

My husband and I haven't settled on a name, and the baby is already overdue. Must we decide on the baby's full name before the birth certificate can be registered?

Not in most states. The time limits during which your child's given names must be recorded vary from 10 days to seven years, depending on where you live.

I am worried about making a mistake on the birth certificate that my child will have to live with forever. What happens if an error appears in my baby's name on the birth certificate?

The best thing to do is to avoid making any mistakes in the first place. Before signing the birth certificate be absolutely sure that it is completely filled out and accurate in every detail. If the birth certificate is processed and you later notice an error, procedures for making the correction vary from state to state. In some states the correction requires only the signatures of the parents, but in other states additional forms must be filled out and documents must be reviewed.

My daughter will be born next month. My husband and I have settled on first and last names, but we don't want to use a middle name. Does my baby have to have a middle name?

Not if you don't want her to. The choice is yours: You can assign your child a middle name (or two), an initial, or skip directly from first to last.

What does my Social Security number mean?

Your Social Security number is like a personal UPC code—it belongs to you and you alone. The first three digits indicate the state where you were born. Originally the lower numbers belonged to Northeasterners and the higher numbers to folks born in the West, but the tidy coding system set up by Social Security was thrown off by some states whose populations have grown so rapidly that they've used up their digits and had to borrow from other states. The middle digits provide an internal Social Security Administration code, and the last four digits are assigned in order of application.

The Social Security Administration has been assigning cards for more than 50 years, but only about one-third of the one billion possible numerical combinations have been used. In about 100 years the early numbers may need to be recycled or another digit or two may need to be added.

What are the legal procedures I should follow if my baby is stillborn or dies shortly after birth?

Your baby's birth—and death—will be recorded by the state department of vital records. If you did not apply for a Social Security number, you do not need to do so. If you already obtained one, the Social Security Administration will be notified of the death automatically so that the number cannot be used illegally.

STEP BY STEP:
YOUR CHILD'S LEGAL ID CHECKLIST

- ❏ Select a name.
- ❏ Fill out and sign the birth certificate.
- ❏ Apply for a Social Security card.
- ❏ Notify your insurance company of the new family member.
- ❏ Store the child's birth certificate and Social Security card in a safe place.

RESOURCES:
WHERE TO GO FOR MORE INFORMATION

BROCHURES

■ For a free copy of the government brochure "Understanding Social Security" contact Consumer Information Center—3B, P.O. Box 100, Pueblo, CO 81002.

ORGANIZATIONS

- **Social Security Administration**: See your Yellow Pages for a local office or call (800) 772-1213.

- **State departments of vital records**: See listing in the Resources section of Chapter 10, "Setting Your Records Straight."

- **Center for Surrogate Parenting**, 8383 Wilshire Blvd., Suite 750, Beverly Hills, CA 90211; (213) 655-1974.

- **Adoptive Families of America**, 3333 Highway 100-N, Minneapolis, MN 55422; (612) 535-4829.

PART 2

MONEY MATTERS

YOUR LITTLE BUNDLE OF JOY will cost a bundle to raise. First, there are the nonnegotiable expenses: the crib, car seat, food, and clothes that kids outgrow long before they outwear. Then, of course, there are the extras, such as the music lessons, braces, pets, and family vacations.

Figures on what it costs to raise a child vary widely. Experts estimate that the cost of bringing up a child from birth to age 18 may range anywhere from $150,000 to $250,000, depending on your lifestyle, habits, and where you live. That figure doesn't include the costs of private schools or four years of college. And it doesn't take into account lost wages for a stay-at-home parent or child-care costs if both parents work away from home.

Just being born is a costly proposition. The final bill can easily exceed $10,000 by the time you cover hospital charges, lab fees, bills from the anesthesiologist, bills from Mom's doctor or midwife, bills from the baby's pediatrician, and so on. The bills mount even faster for cesarean births, since most obstetricians charge more for surgical delivery and hospitals charge for use of operating rooms. The type of health insurance you have and the choices you make about who you want to deliver your baby and where you want your child to be born will have a huge impact on your final bill.

No doubt about it, kids are expensive. But you can overcome parenting price paralysis. Careful planning—for both short-term and long-term goals—is the key to meeting your family's financial obligations without panic.

CHAPTER 4

SECURING YOUR FAMILY'S FUTURE

Buying Life and Disability Insurance

NUTS AND BOLTS

Unless you're an insurance agent, you probably don't like thinking about life and disability insurance. But insurance is a necessary evil—and an important part of protecting your family's financial future.

Though it isn't much fun, buying life and disability insurance should be a high priority for young parents. The first priority should be accumulating a savings nest egg—cash or investments that can be immediately accessed or liquidated without penalty—equal to about six months of the family's income. After this goal is met, parents should buy life and disability insurance. Only after these basics have been covered should money be earmarked for investments, even those as worthy as the college fund.

LIFE INSURANCE

Life insurance is something you buy, then hope you'll never have to use. Life insurance pays the named beneficiary a stated amount, known as the death benefit, when the policyholder dies. People buy life insurance so that their family's minimum needs—the mortgage, child-care expenses, college tuition payments—can be met if a family breadwinner dies prematurely.

Only about two-thirds of all Americans carry life insurance, and most don't have enough. A study by the American Council of Life Insurance showed that more than 40 percent of all adults carry less than $25,000 in life insurance. Not much when you consider the long-term costs of raising and educating children.

To find out if you need life insurance, ask yourself one basic question: Would my spouse, children, parents, or other dependents suffer financial hardship if I die? If you answer yes, you need insurance.

The amount of life insurance you need changes over time. The more children and other dependents you have, the more insurance you need. Some people buy enough insurance that their families won't suffer any decline in standard of living if they die. Others use insurance as a safety net: they carry enough to prevent financial hardship, but not enough to pay for all living expenses. Of course, there is no single right way to plan for your family's future; parents need to make these decisions together.

In the past the nation's 2,000 life insurance companies usually catered to men as the family breadwinners. But today more than half of all mothers with children under age 18 are working outside the home for pay. As a rule, when both parents contribute to the household budget, both should be insured. And in many cases stay-at-home parents need to be insured, too, to cover child-care costs. Homemakers do the cooking and cleaning and child care as well as countless other things to keep the family going, and these tasks must be paid for if neither parent is there to do them.

Your goal is to buy the right amount of insurance—not too much or too little. You don't want your loved ones to have to struggle financially when you're gone, but you don't want the family to struggle financially by paying too high premiums for too much insurance while you're alive, either.

That's why you need to reassess your insurance needs frequently. As children get older and the family wealth increases, you will probably need less insurance. Even though your salary may go up, your insurance needs will go down because you're buying insurance to cover fewer years of expenses. Remember, you're not insuring your lifetime earnings, you're insuring the cost of raising your children and putting them through college. Because life insurance needs vary with time, you should review your life insurance coverage every two or three years. Of course, you should also adjust your coverage under certain circumstances, including:

- The birth or adoption of a baby;
- Marriage or divorce;
- Purchase of a house;
- Taking on a second mortgage, home-equity loan, or other major debt;
- Death of a family member;
- Changed careers or jobs;
- Retirement.

Types of Life Insurance

Though any life insurance salesperson can tell you about the unique features of a particular company's policies, there are two main types of life insurance: term insurance and cash-value insurance. Term insurance offers insurance protection for a set period of time—and that's it. Cash-value policies package insurance coverage together with a savings plan that has a cash value (hence the name). Here's a summary of these basic types of insurance policies:

Term Insurance. With term insurance the policyholder pays for protection for a specific number of years, usually one, three, or five years. If the policyholder dies while the policy is in force, the company pays the beneficiary the amount stated in the policy. If the policyholder lives beyond the term of the insurance, the insurance company pays nothing.

Term insurance is cheaper than cash-value insurance for the same amount of insurance protection because it pays only for death benefits: there is no investment component, no cash value, and hence no high premium. The difference in premiums for the two types of insurance can be significant. For example, a 25-year-old man would pay $250 the first year for $250,000 in annually renewable term insurance or $2,750 per year for the same amount of coverage from a traditional whole-life policy.

While the premiums for term insurance are low in the beginning, they steadily rise with age. The premiums go up with each passing year because a policyholder is statistically more likely to die as he or she grows older. During the early years the premiums tend to rise relatively slowly, but by age 45 to 50 the premium costs start to climb steeply.

In addition, some people may find it more difficult to qualify for term insurance as they grow older. Most insurance companies require that policyholders get medical examinations before being considered eligible to buy insurance. The insurance company wants to make sure you're healthy before taking a risk on writing a policy on your life. If you develop a health problem, the company may not want to renew the policy, even at the higher rate. That's why it's a good idea to look for a term policy that is renewable.

Beyond standard term insurance, there are two other types: decreasing and increasing term insurance. Decreasing term insurance pays less and less to the beneficiary as time passes, though the premium stays the same. This type of term insurance gives you the most protection at the beginning of the policy and less toward the end. It makes sense for people who expect that their total family expenses will decrease over time, often because their home mortgage will be paid off.

Increasing term insurance sometimes includes an "inflation guard" or "cost-of-living" provision, which increases the insurance benefit over time. Of course, with increasing term insurance, the premiums increase with coverage increases.

Cash-Value Insurance. Cash-value life insurance policies combine traditional life insurance with a tax-deferred savings plan. Part of your premium goes to pay for life insurance and part goes into a cash reserve, which accumulates as an investment. The savings are yours, even if you cancel the life insurance policy.

You can also borrow money from the insurance company at a rate of interest stated in the policy, using the cash value you have built up as collateral for the loan. Even after you borrow against the policy, you must continue to pay the premiums to keep the policy in force. If you die before paying back the loan, the insurance company will reduce the amount it pays your beneficiary by the amount outstanding on the loan. And if your circumstances change and you no longer want to

PROS AND CONS OF CASH-VALUE POLICIES

Pros

- The cash invested in the policy earns interest tax-free until the policy is cashed in.
- The cash value goes to the policyholder when the policy is terminated.
- Loans against a cash-value policy can be taken at lower-than-market interest rates.
- The cash value can be used to pay life insurance premiums.

Cons

- Premiums for cash-value policies are initially much higher than those for term insurance. (You could buy term insurance and take the difference between the annual premium for a cash-value policy and the annual premium for the term policy and invest the difference yourself. In effect, you would be creating your own cash-value program.)
- Cash value builds very slowly for the first few years.
- Some cash-value policies earn low rates of return.
- The rates of return are not guaranteed; in many cases the rate policyholders earn depends on the investment expertise of the insur-

pay for insurance protection, you can cancel the insurance policy and take your accumulated savings, known as the cash surrender value.

Though there are subtle differences between policies offered by different companies, there are three main types of cash-value policies: whole life insurance, universal life insurance, and variable life insurance.

Whole-life insurance pays a specified amount to the beneficiary when the policyholder dies, just like term insurance. But unlike term insurance, the policy lasts the policyholder's whole life—or as long as the policyholder pays the premiums.

Whole-life insurance, sometimes called straight life insurance, also builds cash value over time. Whole-life insurance costs more than comparable amounts of term insurance in the early years, though with most policies the rates don't increase as the policyholder gets older. Policyholders who buy whole-life insurance when they are young initially pay more than required for the amount of insurance protection they are buying; that's how they build cash value in the policy. As policyholders get older, however, they pay a lower premium than would be required for term insurance.

Whole-life policies allow policyholders to borrow up to the full cash value of the policy. The advantage: The interest rates charged by the insurance company are usually lower than bank loan rates. Another bonus: If you no longer want to pay the premiums, you can authorize the insurance company to take money from the cash value of the policy to keep the insurance in force.

Universal life insurance differs from whole-life insurance in that it separates the insurance cost from the savings part of the policy. With a universal policy the savings part of the premium is invested by the insurance company in securities and investments that earn higher interest rates than those paid by the whole-life investments.

Within certain bounds set out in your policy, it's up to you to decide how much you want to put into savings. Once you've invested enough money in the policy, the cash in the savings portion can be used to pay the insurance premiums. When the policyholder dies, the beneficiary collects both the death benefit and the cash value of the policy.

Variable life insurance works a lot like universal insurance, except that the policyholder is able to decide which investments are purchased with the cash-value dollars. Policyholders can choose from a number of investments, including stock funds, corporate and government bond funds, and money market funds. Most companies allow policyholders to change their investment choices, usually at two periods each year. In most cases variable life insurance costs somewhat more than whole-life and universal insurance.

Keeping Your Options Open

When shopping for a life insurance policy, you will be offered a number of special options or riders, all available for an extra fee. These are a few of the most common options:

Double indemnity. This coverage, also called an accidental-death rider, basically doubles your coverage if you die in an accident. If you pay still more, you can triple the coverage. Most companies offer this coverage only for people under age 65.

As a rule, double-indemnity riders state that death must occur within a certain time after the accidental injury, usually 90 days. The policy doesn't pay if someone is killed in a war or riot or if the death was not accidental. The costs vary with age: a 35-year-old buying a $100,000 whole-life policy would pay about $70 per year for coverage, whereas a 50-year-old with the same policy would pay about $75.

Waiver of premium. This is a relatively inexpensive way to make sure your insurance premium will be paid if you become disabled. This is not to be confused with disability insurance: waiver-of-premium pays only for the life insurance premium, whereas disability insurance helps to replace lost income.

Companies have different waiting periods before the waiver-of-premium coverage kicks in: some companies cover premiums after three months; others wait until six months after a disabling accident or illness. Most companies will not offer this coverage to people older than 60.

Cost-of-living rider. This coverage gives you the right to buy additional insurance coverage to keep up with the cost of living, without having to prove you're in good physical condition. Some companies limit the amount of extra coverage you can buy this way, often to 10 percent of the face value of the policy.

Guaranteed insurability. This coverage guarantees that you will be able to buy additional insurance in the future without passing another medical exam. Most companies offer guaranteed insurability only to people under age 40.

Guaranteed insurability won't help you qualify for the policy in the first place. When you initially apply for coverage, all companies will ask you a series of questions about your health: Do you smoke? Drink? Have AIDS? And many will require a medical exam.

If a company is suspicious of anything written on the application, a company representative may check to see if you have a file at the Medical Information Bureau, a computer data bank with information on life, health, and disability insurance policies. If you lie on an insurance application and you die within two years, the policy may not be in force.

Term-insurance rider. This is a combination of term insurance and a cash-value policy. Since many families can't afford to buy enough insurance if they buy a cash-value policy, this rider allows them to buy some term insurance, too. Most companies limit the amount of term insurance that can be purchased, usually to three times the basic amount of the cash-value policy.

LIFE INSURANCE AND TAXES

Life insurance proceeds aren't tax-free. The situation is confusing because although you could be the beneficiary of a $1 million life insurance policy and not pay a penny in federal *income* tax, you'd still face a stiff federal *estate* tax bill.

You may not have to worry about estate taxes. If the value of your estate—including the proceeds from your life insurance policy—falls below the $600,000 mark, you won't have to pay any estate taxes. However, if your life is heavily insured, the proceeds of your life insurance policy could push your estate above the $600,000 line, which means that your heirs would have to pay estate taxes.

You can avoid the estate tax by keeping the insurance proceeds out of your taxable estate. There are two main ways of doing this: you can give your insurance policy to someone else, or you can transfer it to a trust.

Don't assume that you're safe because your spouse is the beneficiary and the money won't be taxed because of the marital deduction. (There is no limit to the value of an estate that can pass to a spouse tax-free.) You haven't solved the problem; you've only delayed dealing with it. The money won't be taxed when it passes to your spouse, but it will be taxed when it passes to your children.

You can avoid this situation by transferring ownership to your spouse and naming the children as beneficiaries. Since you no longer own the policy, it is not included in your taxable estate.

The paperwork involved in changing ownership is simple: all you have to do is fill out a short form provided by your insurance company. The downside (there's always a downside) is that you will have to sign away all rights to your policies: the gift must be absolute and irrevocable. You can no longer change your beneficiaries, and in the case of policies with cash value, you transfer the right to borrow against them or cash them in. And if you want to make a switch, be aware that you can't procrastinate over this ownership transfer until you are on your deathbed. If the deed is done within three years of your demise, the money is counted as part of your estate no matter who owns the policy.

Think through the consequences carefully with a financial adviser before signing away an insurance policy. If it has cash value of more than $10,000, your estate may have to pay a gift tax on a transfer to anyone other than your spouse.

Taxes aren't the only consideration. Once you give the policy to your spouse, you can't get it back, even if you divorce. As owner, your spouse has the right to cash in the policy or change the beneficiary, potentially leaving your children high and dry.

If you have a lot of money, the best way to avoid estate taxes and to protect your children as beneficiaries may be to set up an irrevocable life insurance trust. When you die, the trust collects the money and the trustee you name in the will distributes it to your beneficiaries. The drawback is that such a trust is expensive to set up and maintain. Many estate planners recommend irrevocable life insurance trusts only for estates exceeding $2 million (see Chapter 1).

Guaranteed renewability. Renewable term insurance is somewhat more expensive than regular term—about 25 cents to 60 cents more per $1,000 of coverage—but it's generally worth it. With such a policy the company must renew your insurance at the end of the term at your request unless you haven't paid your premium. Guaranteed insurability allows you to buy more insurance; guaranteed renewability allows you to renew the policy you already have.

DISABILITY INSURANCE

Though you probably don't think of it as an asset, your ability to earn a living is likely the single most valuable resource you possess. Don't think of your annual wages alone; consider your lifetime earning potential. It adds up fast, doesn't it?

The purpose of disability insurance is to protect your earning power in case it is interrupted due to accident or illness. The disability wouldn't have to put you in a wheelchair for life; it could be caused by a heart attack, a stroke, cancer, a car accident—any event that affects your health and your ability to earn a living.

Unlike life insurance, which you buy to protect your family after you're gone, disability insurance is something you buy to protect both your family and yourself. After all, if you were to become disabled, your family would have to get by without your income, and at the same time the family budget would be strained by additional medical bills and other expenses related to your disability.

Disability insurance is just as important as life insurance. In fact, the odds of your being disabled for an extended period before you reach age 65 are greater than the odds of your dying before then. For that reason, buying disability insurance makes sense for anyone who earns a good wage and can afford to pay the premiums, although most people don't carry enough individual disability insurance to offer adequate protection. About 80 percent of all workers under age 65 have some disability insurance—usually from an employer plan or from the government—but in many cases the coverage is only short term, with benefits payable for two years or less. Only 20 percent of all workers have long-term disability insurance, and only long-term policies provide long-term security against the possibility of financial disaster.

Don't count on Social Security to cushion the blow if you become disabled. Yes, Social Security provides disability insurance for people who become disabled before age 65, but you should be aware that 70 percent of all Social Security disability claims are rejected. If you want to ensure financial security, you probably need to buy a separate disability insurance policy.

How Much Disability Insurance Is Enough?

It's easy to buy too much life insurance—some insurance agents will even try to get you to do so—but it's impossible to buy too much disability insurance. You can't buy a disability insurance policy to cover more than your gross income; otherwise, you could make money by being disabled. Most companies limit coverage to 65 to 85 percent of your gross income and will decrease your benefit if you'll make more money disabled than you did when you worked.

Disability insurance allows you to collect a monthly check equal to a certain percentage of your base salary at the time you became disabled. For example, if you owned a policy that pays 60 percent of your salary and you were disabled while earning $2,000 a month, you would collect $1,200 a month in payments.

Since disability benefits you buy yourself are tax-free, you need to buy only enough insurance to replace your take-home pay. When deciding how much insurance to buy, you should also take into consideration any Social Security benefits or other government programs (such as Veterans Administration pension disability benefits, Civil Service disability benefits, and federal and state compensation programs) you might be entitled to. Social Security disability benefits for the handicapped aren't taxed; neither are benefits when you buy a disability policy and pay the premiums yourself. However, if your employer buys a policy for you, those benefits are taxed.

Don't count on Social Security benefits alone to get you through a crisis. The eligibility requirements are stringent: you must have a serious health problem that produces total disability of more than a year or that will result in death. Payments are also made only in the case of complete disability, meaning you must be unable to work in any job. Even if you met those requirements, you would have to wait at least six months before collecting your first check. (This is why having a nest egg of six months' salary is so important.)

Since the amount of disability insurance you can buy depends on your salary, you should review your policy and adjust your coverage as your salary increases. Many companies sell an option giving you the right to buy more insurance at certain specified times stated in the policy.

The price of disability insurance is based primarily on sex, age, and occupation. Women pay more than men, older people pay more than younger people, and people in high-risk occupations pay more than those in low-risk occupations. The rates aren't based on any unfair bias but on raw actuarial data. An office worker is statistically less likely to be injured than a construction worker or circus performer.

Most policies offer level premiums, meaning the amount you'll pay now is what you'll pay next year and the year after, and so on, as long as there is no change in the level of benefits you want. So it pays to buy disability insurance when you're young to lock in the low premium. For example, if you bought a disability insurance policy when you were 30, you might pay $650 a year, but if you waited until age 45, the cost might be $1,200. If you kept the policy in force until age 65, your total payments would be less if you first bought coverage when you were younger: $22,750 if you bought at age 30 or $24,000 if you bought at age 45.

Other Factors to Consider

Shopping for disability insurance can be tricky. There are a number of variables to consider and options to weigh. Before buying a policy, make sure you understand exactly what's covered, when the coverage starts, and how long the coverage lasts. When comparing policies, ask the following questions:

Is it short-term or long-term coverage? Short-term policies pay benefits for up to two years; long-term policies provide benefits for longer periods, usually five years, until age 65, or for life. For most people coverage to age 65 makes the most sense. Policies for shorter terms (such as one, two, or five years) cost a lot less, but they don't protect against the kind of catastrophic, long-term loss of income that can wipe out your family.

Is the policy noncancelable? A disability policy should include a guarantee that as long as you pay your premiums on time, the insurance company can't cancel it before it runs out.

Is it guaranteed renewable? You should have the right to renew your policy on the same terms and at the same rates until you reach age 65. (No insurance company guarantees renewal after 65.) You should be able to renew even if you change jobs, lose your job, or take a cut in pay.

Companies generally offer one of three types of renewability provisions: class cancelable, guaranteed renewable, and guaranteed renewable and noncancelable. *Class cancelable* means the company can cancel an entire group of policyholders (such as all policies written before 1970 or all policies written in Vermont). A person whose policy is canceled must switch to another company, probably at a greater cost since he or she would be older when applying. *Guaranteed renewable* policies can't be canceled, but the company can raise the premiums. The safest policies are *guaranteed renewable and noncancelable*,

DO YOU NEED AN INSURANCE AGENT?

If you use an insurance agent, you want one you can trust with your life—or at least your life insurance. When considering what kind of agent you need—and whether you need an agent at all—keep in mind that each option has its pros and cons:

- **Exclusive agents** work for just one company.
  PROS: Policies are somewhat less expensive than those sold by independent agents due to the commission structure. To lure the agents, insurance companies pay higher commissions—and charge you a higher price—for policies sold by independent agents.
  CONS: You'll have to do more footwork to compare policies between companies.

- **Independent agents** work for a number of companies.
  PROS: The agent can show you a wider variety of policies.
  CONS: Policy prices may be higher since the companies pay more to lure independent agents to their products.

- **Insurance brokers** sell insurance as well as other financial products.

  PROS: One-stop shopping for all your financial and insurance needs.
  CONS: Because they are financial generalists, brokers may not know as much about life and disability insurance as an insurance agent.

- **Shopping for yourself** allows you to cut out the middleman and buy direct from the insurance company.
  PROS: You can save the cost of the commission.
  CONS: You need to know exactly what kind of policy and coverage you need. Some companies won't sell to individuals; others will provide only term insurance, no cash-value policies.

Before buying from any insurance agent, ask about the commission structure. If the agent balks, walk. The agent is asking for you to be forthcoming about your financial circumstances, and you deserve the same respect.

Also, check with the state department of insurance to find out if there have been any complaints filed against the agent you are considering. The agent should be on file, since all insurance agents and brokers must be licensed by the state.

which are policies that cannot be canceled, with premiums that cannot be raised.

How does the policy define the term disability? All insurance companies agree that you are disabled if you're under a doctor's care and unable to perform the duties of your job. However, some policies stipulate that you can't collect benefits if you could be employed in any other job. Other policies say you can collect as long as you've suffered a loss of income, whether you're working in another job or not.

Most companies won't cover disability caused by acts of war or self-inflicted injuries. Some exclude disability following organ transplant or cosmetic surgery.

Should I insure my occupation as well as my income? This provision clarifies the issue of disability. If a brain surgeon who makes $500,000 a year suffers a stroke and cannot operate again, although she can hold down an office job that pays $40,000 a year, is she disabled? It depends on the company's definition of disability. A so-called own-occupation

COMPARISON-SHOP BY PHONE

Several companies are willing to do your insurance shopping for you. You provide some personal information, such as your age, health, and amount of insurance required, and the company provides a free list of four or five of the least-expensive policies among those monitored by the service. Most monitor about 200 companies, all of which pay commissions to the company. For more information, contact:

- **SelectQuote Insurance Services**, 595 Market Street, 5th Floor, San Francisco, CA 94105; (800) 343-1985, (415) 543-7338.
- **InsuranceQuote Services**, 3200 N. Dobson Road, Building C, Chandler, AZ 85224; (800) 972-1104, (602) 345-7241.
- **TermQuote**, 3445 South Dixie Drive, Dayton, OH 45439; (800) 444-8376, (513) 294-8989.
- **USAA Life**, USAA Building, 9800 Fredricksburg Road, San Antonio, TX 78288; (800) 531-8000, (210) 498-8000.
- **Insurance Information Inc.**, Cobblestone Court, #23, Route 134, South Dennis, MA 02660, (800) 472-5800.

contract specifies that the person must be able to return to work in the original occupation at a salary in the same ballpark as before.

An own-occupation contract boosts your premium considerably, and for many people it is an unnecessary frill. An alternative: an income-replacement policy, which covers you whether you can work full time, part time, or not at all. It simply replaces a percentage of the income you have lost because of the disability.

Will preexisting conditions be covered? Some companies won't cover a preexisting condition for the first year of the policy; others will. Find out how each company defines and handles preexisting conditions.

Do the benefits have cost-of-living adjustments? Adding a cost-of-living adjustment (COLA) can increase premium costs by a whopping 25 to 30 percent. It's expensive coverage that only pays if you're disabled for a long time. Compare COLAs carefully: some are based on a guaranteed simple rate, such as 4 percent or 7 percent annually, while others are linked to the consumer price index (with or without a cap or a guaranteed minimum).

How long is the waiting period before I can collect? You'll have to decide when you want the company to start paying benefits—at 30 days, 60 days, 90 days, 6 months, or 1 year after you become disabled. The longer you're willing to wait to collect benefits, the lower your premiums will be. If at all possible, select a waiting period of at least two or three months: waiting 90 days instead of 30 slashes your basic premiums by almost 50 percent.

Does the policy cover pregnancy? Ask to be sure. Some companies cover only complications from pregnancy, such as hypertension, placenta previa, and other problems that require bed rest; others cover normal pregnancy but throw in a 90-day waiting period, which could mean that by relying on this policy, you'd lose a lot of income.

ISSUES TO DISCUSS:
WHAT PARENTS SHOULD TALK ABOUT

- ❑ How much life insurance do we need?
- ❑ What kind of policy?
- ❑ Whom should we name as beneficiaries?
- ❑ Who should "own" the policy?
- ❑ Do we need disability insurance? How much?
- ❑ Will our insurance policies result in taxable income for our estate?
- ❑ How frequently will we review and update our policies?

QUESTIONS & ANSWERS

Should I buy life insurance for my child?

No. First of all, statistically your child is not apt to die. Second, you do not need to insure your child because your child does not contribute to the family income. Of course, losing a child would be an almost unbearable emotional hardship, but it would probably not be a financial hardship. For most families it makes more sense to use the money that would be spent on the child's policy and to increase the amount of coverage on the family breadwinners.

If you're considering a cash-value life insurance policy as an investment for your child, that's another matter. Parents who are unable to discipline themselves to save regularly may benefit from the forced savings required of cash-value policies. Others may be attracted to the tax-deferred feature of cash-value life insurance, depending on their tax circumstances. If you are interested in cash-value insurance for your child, you should assess the merits of the insurance policy as an investment, disregarding the insurance protection.

What is the difference between renewable and level term life insurance?

Renewable term insurance can be renewed year after year, but the premiums go up each year. Level-premium policies provide fixed rates for the entire term (say, five or 10 years). With level premiums the initial premiums are higher, but they don't go up over time. When comparing policies, price out the options. In many cases, over a 10- or 15-year period a level-premium policy may be cheaper than a renewable policy.

I have tried to buy life insurance from several companies, but I have been repeatedly turned down. What can I do?

You may be among the approximately 3 percent of life insurance applicants who are considered substandard risks. About 80 percent of these high-risk people have physical problems, such as heart disease, obesity, and high blood pressure, that make them uninsurable. The other 20 percent are usually disqualified due to occupational hazards, excessive traveling, or foreign residence.

Being a substandard risk doesn't doom you to the realm of the uninsured forever. You may be able to qualify for group insurance policies through a fraternal, social, or professional group; these group policies don't require individual assessment of insurability. Also, some individual insurance may be available without a medical examination, but the limits of coverage are usually quite low.

If you strike out again, contact an insurance agent who specializes in obtaining life and disability insurance for substandard risks. Ask your local insurance agent or the state insurance department for leads on tracking down a specialist.

How should I go about finding out if my insurance company is in good financial shape?

Before buying a life or disability insurance policy, you want to make sure your insurer is solvent. Five major ratings services—A. M. Best, Standard & Poor's, Duff & Phelps, Moody's, and Weiss Research—assess the financial stability of insurance companies. While a high rating doesn't necessarily ensure that a company will remain strong, it makes no sense to make a long-term financial commitment to a company that isn't doing well.

Each rating service uses a letter grade to measure the company's security, but be aware that the companies don't use the same scale. For example, Best rates from A++, A+, A . . . ; Duff & Phelps from AAA, AA+, AA . . . ; Moody's from Aaa, Aa1, Aa2 . . . ; Standard & Poor's from AAA, AA+, AA . . . ; and Weiss from A+, A, A– . . . . An insurance company earning the grade A would have earned a second-best rating from Weiss, third best from Best, and fifth best from Standard & Poor's and Duff & Phelps.

You can go to the library and look the ratings up in a number of financial service books (the librarian should be able to help), or you can call the ratings services directly. Standard & Poor's will provide the rating free of charge if you call (212) 208-1527. Best will provide an oral report if you call (900) 420-0400; cost: $2.50 per minute. Weiss provides an oral letter-grade report over the phone for $15; the number is (800) 289-9222. A one-page written report costs $25, a detailed report, $45.

My life insurance policy offers a "living needs" benefit. What is this?

It's a rider—usually provided free of cost—that allows you to take a percentage of your death benefit before you die. In most cases the living-needs rider is triggered when you become terminally ill and are expected to die within 12 months. Most companies require that you allow a doctor appointed by the insurance company to certify your condition.

Some living-needs policies permit you to take a percentage of the death benefit, usually 25 to 40 percent, and the company computes interest on the amount taken. When you die, your beneficiaries receive the value of the policy minus the amount advanced and the added interest. Other companies use a "discount method" and deduct the interest in advance, based on your life expectancy. If you were to collect $30,000, the company might only give you $27,000, claiming the rest as forgone interest.

My life insurance agent is pushing a cash-value policy. Why?

Because agents make more money selling cash-value insurance. Insurance agents who collect commissions on their sales have a built-in incentive to sell certain policies. Some agents are paid a commission of up to 100 percent of the first-year premium when they sell a whole-life policy but only 70 percent of a much smaller premium when they sell term insurance. As a result many agents discourage customers from buying term insurance by referring to it disparagingly as "temporary," while cash-value insurance is labeled "permanent."

What is credit life insurance, and do I need it?

Credit life insurance is a life insurance policy designed to cover the unpaid balance on a particular loan in the event of the borrower's death. Don't buy credit life insurance unless you know you're about to die; it's almost always outrageously expensive. And it's unnecessary if you have enough life insurance in the first place. If you need extra coverage, skip the credit insurance and spend the money on a term insurance policy that will cover the amount you owe.

I have lost my life insurance policy. What should I do?

You can request a policy search form by contacting the American Council of Life Insurance, Attention: Policy Search Department, 1001 Pennsylvania Avenue NW, Washington, DC 20004. Or call the National Insurance Consumer Helpline at (800) 942-4242. Be sure to include a stamped, self-addressed, business-size envelope with your request.

What is a return-of-premium disability policy?

It's a gimmick to get you to spend more money than you need to on disability insurance. A return-of-premium policy promises to return a portion of your money, say 80 percent, if you don't file a claim. These policies tend to be much more expensive then traditional policies—as much as 50 percent more. And you won't necessarily get your money back. If you file a claim, the amount you get back is reduced. Many policies also have "surrender charges" if you try to get your hands on the money before age 65. As a rule, if you need disability insurance, you should buy it and hope you won't need to use it. Don't spend more than you need to and hope that you will one day get part of the money back.

I recently gave up smoking. Will my life insurance rates go down?

Probably. Many companies offer discounts to policyholders who are nonsmokers and to people who take part in regular physical exercise. Nonsmokers often pay 40 to 50 percent less than smokers. Ask your insurance agent if you qualify for a discount now that you've kicked the habit.

How can I find out if a cash-value policy is a good investment?

It's tough to compare life insurance policies. The National Insurance Consumers Organization will do the job for you, for a fee. For more information and a complete evaluation of various policies contact the National Insurance Consumers Organization, Rate of Return Service, P.O. Box 15492, Alexandria, VA 22309; (703) 549-8050. Cost: $30 for the first policy and $20 for each additional policy.

The company I work for offers a small death-benefit-only life insurance policy. What is the purpose of this coverage?

Many employers provide a minimal life insurance policy as part of a basic benefits package. This is basically a way that your employer can help your heirs pay for your funeral. This $5,000 or $10,000 policy probably isn't going to go very far if you have children to raise and put through college; you probably need additional insurance.

What is "key man insurance"?

Key man insurance is typically purchased by a business to insure the lives of those employees who are essential to the enterprise. For example, the owners of a restaurant may want to buy insurance for the famous chef who works for them: if the chef were to die, the value of the business would decline. In some cases a token benefit is paid to the family as well, but the primary purpose of key man insurance is to protect the business.

STEP BY STEP:
LIFE INSURANCE CHECKLIST

- ❏ Use the work sheet on page 78 to estimate the amount of life insurance coverage needed for you and your spouse.
- ❏ Decide what type of life insurance you can afford to buy.
- ❏ Select a beneficiary for your life insurance policy. Consider the tax implications of your decision (see page 64).
- ❏ Estimate the amount of disability insurance you and your spouse need; be sure to check any policy your employer may hold for you.
- ❏ Decide what kind of coverage you need, including how long you want the coverage, when you want payments to begin, and what amount of income you want to have insured.

❑ Collect rates from at least five companies for both your life insurance and disability policies.

❑ If you need help analyzing the policies, obtain a low-cost analysis of the policies from an independent organization.

❑ Buy the policies and store them in a safe place.

❑ When you pay your premium or at least once a year, consider whether you need to reassess your life insurance and disability insurance needs. Keep in mind that your insurance needs are apt to decline as you get older.

HOW MUCH DISABILITY INSURANCE DO YOU NEED?

To find out how much disability insurance you need:

First

Take your income reported on last year's federal income tax return and subtract the amount of taxes and Social Security paid. Divide this number by 12. This is the amount of monthly pay you will attempt to replace.

$_____

Second

Make a list of all existing coverage. Include Social Security benefits, other government programs, and employer disability coverage. Estimate on a monthly basis. (For a free estimate of government disability benefits, if any, call 800-772-1213.)

$_____

Third

Subtract the amount of existing coverage from the monthly pay estimated in step 1. This is the amount of disability insurance you need.

$_____

HOW MUCH LIFE INSURANCE DO YOU NEED?

STEP 1: Make a list of your expenses.

One-time Expenses

Federal estate taxes (*see Chapter 1*) _____

State inheritance taxes _____

Probate costs (*if unsure, estimate at 4 percent of assets
   passing through probate*) _____

Funeral and burial costs (*most cost about $7,500*) _____

PLUS +

Ongoing Expenses

Family living expenses (*You can either calculate using
   your family budget or use 75 percent of your take-home
   pay as a rule of thumb*) _____

Child-care costs _____

College tuition _____

Other debts _____

TOTAL FUTURE EXPENSES = $ _____

STEP 2: Determine your future income.

Spouse's income _____

Dividends, royalties, interest on investments _____

Real estate _____

Pensions _____

Social Security (*To obtain an estimate of your survivors'
   benefits, request the "Personal Earnings and Benefits Estimate
   Statement" by calling 800-937-2000*) _____

Retirement plans and IRAs _____

Existing life insurance (*such as plans through an employer*) _____

TOTAL FUTURE INCOME = $ _____

STEP 3: Calculate the amount of insurance you need by
subtracting your total future income from your total
future expenses.

TOTAL FUTURE EXPENSES = $ _____

TOTAL FUTURE INCOME − $ _____

TOTAL AMOUNT OF INSURANCE YOU NEED = $ _____

RESOURCES:
WHERE TO GO FOR MORE INFORMATION

BOOKS

■ **Taking the Bite Out of Insurance: How to Save Money on Life Insurance**, by James Hunt. Cost: $13.95; includes shipping and handling. Contact: National Insurance Consumer Organization, P.O. Box 15492, Alexandria, VA 22309; (703) 549-8050.

■ **Life Insurance: How to Buy the Right Policy from the Right Company at the Right Price**, by Trudy Lieberman. Cost: $11.95, plus $2.50 shipping. Contact: Consumer Reports Books at (800) 272-0722.

BROCHURES AND PAMPHLETS

■ "Insurance Checklist," by the American Association of Retired Persons. Cost: Free. Contact: AARP, 601 E Street NW, Washington, DC 20049; (202) 434-2277.

■ "Buyer's Guide to Insurance: What the Companies Won't Tell You," by the National Insurance Consumers Organization. Cost: $3.00, plus a self-addressed stamped envelope. Contact: NICO, 121 N. Payne Street, Alexandria, VA 22314; (703) 549-8050.

■ "A Consumer's Guide to Life Insurance," by the American Council of Life Insurance. Cost: Free. Contact: American Council of Life Insurance, 1001 Pennsylvania Ave. NW, Suite 500 South, Washington, DC 20004; (202) 624-2000.

■ "Tips on Life Insurance," by the Better Business Bureau. Cost: $1.00, plus a self-addressed, stamped, business-size envelope. Contact: Council of Better Business Bureaus, Department 023, 4200 Wilson Blvd., Suite 800, Arlington, VA 22203; (703) 276-0100.

■ "A Consumer's Guide to Life Insurance," by the U.S. Department of Agriculture. Cost: Free. Contact: Consumer Information Center—3B, P.O. Box 100, Pueblo, CO 81002.

ORGANIZATIONS AND HOTLINES

- **National Insurance Consumer Helpline,** (800) 942-4242.

- **National Insurance Consumers Organization**, P.O. Box 15492, Alexandria, VA 22309; (703) 549-8050.

STATE INSURANCE DEPARTMENTS

Insurance is regulated on a state-by-state basis. Though the specific functions of insurance departments vary from state to state, all departments monitor the financial condition of every company doing business in the state. The insurance departments also license companies and agents, approve policy wording and rates, and address consumer complaints.

ALABAMA Insurance Department
P.O. Box 303351
Montgomery, AL 36130-3351
(205) 269-3550

ALASKA Division of Insurance
P.O. Box 110805
Juneau, AK 99811-0805
(907) 465-2515

ARIZONA Insurance Department
2910 North 44th Street, Suite 210
Phoenix, AZ 85018
(602) 912-8400

ARKANSAS Insurance Department
1123 South University, Suite 400
Little Rock, AK 72204-1699
(501) 686-2900

CALIFORNIA Insurance Commission
100 Van Ness Avenue
San Francisco, CA 94102
(800) 927-4357

COLORADO Division of Insurance
1560 Broadway, Suite 850
Denver, CO 80202
(303) 894-7499

CONNECTICUT Insurance
  Department
P.O. Box 816
Hartford, CT 06142-0816
(203) 297-3800

DELAWARE Insurance Department
841 Silver Lake Blvd.
Dover, DE 19901
(302) 739-4251

DISTRICT OF COLUMBIA
  Insurance Department
441 4th Street NW, 8th Floor North
Washington, DC 20001
(202) 727-7424

FLORIDA Insurance Department
State Capitol, Plaza Level 11
Tallahassee, FL 32399-0300
(904) 922-3100; (800) 342-2762

GEORGIA Insurance Commission
2 Martin Luther King Jr. Drive
Floyd Memorial Building
716 West Tower
Atlanta, GA 30334
(404) 656-2056

HAWAII Insurance Division
P.O. Box 3614
Honolulu, HA 96811
(808) 586-2790

IDAHO Insurance Department
700 West State Street, 3rd Floor
Boise, ID 83720
(208) 334-2250

ILLINOIS Insurance Department
320 W. Washington Street, 4th Floor
Springfield, IL 62767
(217) 782-4515

INDIANA Insurance Department
311 West Washington Street,
    Suite 300
Indianapolis, IN 46204-2787
(317) 232-2385

IOWA Insurance Commission
Lucas State Office Building,
    6th Floor
Des Moines, IA 50319
(515) 281-5705

KANSAS Insurance Department
420 South West Ninth Street
Topeka, KS 66612
(913) 296-7801; (800) 432-2484

KENTUCKY Insurance Department
215 West Main Street
P.O. Box 517
Frankfort, KY 40602
(502) 564-3630

LOUISIANA Insurance Commission
950 North 5th Street
Baton Rouge, LA 70802
(504) 342-5900

MAINE Bureau of Insurance
State House, Station 34
Augusta, ME 04333
(207) 582-8707

MARYLAND Insurance Division
501 St. Paul Place, 7th Floor South
Baltimore, MD 21202
(410) 333-6300

MASSACHUSETTS Division
    of Insurance
470 Atlantic Ave.
Boston, MA 02210-2223
(617) 521-7794

MICHIGAN Insurance Bureau
P.O. Box 30220
Lansing, MI 48909
(517) 373-9273

MINNESOTA Department
of Commerce
Insurance Division
133 East 7th Street
St. Paul, MN 55101
(612) 296-6848

MISSISSIPPI Department
of Insurance
1804 Walter Sillers Building
Jackson, MS 39205
(601) 359-3569

MISSOURI Insurance Department
301 W. High Street, Room 630
P.O. Box 690
Jefferson City, MO 65102-0690
(314) 751-4126

MONTANA Insurance Securities
Department
P.O. Box 4009
Helena, MT 59604
(406) 444-2040; (800) 332-6148

NEBRASKA Insurance Department
Terminal Building
941 O Street, Suite 400
Lincoln, NE 68508
(402) 471-2201

NEVADA Insurance Commission
1665 Hot Springs Road, Suite 152
Carson City, NV 89706
(702) 687-4270

NEW HAMPSHIRE Insurance
Department
169 Manchester Street
Concord, NH 03301
(603) 271-2261; (800) 852-3416

NEW JERSEY Insurance Department
CN-329
Trenton, NJ 08625
(609) 292-5363

NEW MEXICO Insurance
Department
P.O. Drawer 1269
Santa Fe, NM 87504-1269
(505) 827-4545

NEW YORK Insurance Department
160 W. Broadway
New York, NY 10013
(212) 602-0429

NORTH CAROLINA Department
of Insurance
Dobbs Building, P.O. Box 26387
Raleigh, NC 27611
(919) 733-7349; (800) 662-7777

NORTH DAKOTA Insurance
Department
Capitol Building, 5th Floor
600 East Blvd.
Bismarck, ND 58505-0320
(701) 224-2440; (800) 247-0560

OHIO Department of Insurance
2100 Stella Court
Columbus, OH 43266-0566
(614) 644-2658

OKLAHOMA Insurance Department
P.O. Box 53408
Oklahoma City, OK 73152
(405) 521-2828

OREGON Insurance Division
440 Labor and Industries Building
Salem, OR 97310
(503) 378-4271

PENNSYLVANIA Insurance
 Department
1326 Strawberry Square, 13th Floor
Harrisburg, PA 17120
(717) 787-5173

RHODE ISLAND Department of
 Business Regulation
Insurance Division
233 Richmond Street
Providence, RI 02903-4233
(401) 277-2246

SOUTH CAROLINA Insurance
 Department
1612 Marion Street
P.O. Box 100105
Columbia, SC 29202-3105
(803) 737-6160

SOUTH DAKOTA Division
 of Insurance
Insurance Building
910 E. Sioux Avenue
Pierre, SD 57501
(605) 773-3563

TENNESSEE Insurance Department
500 James Robertson Parkway,
 5th Floor
Nashville, TN 37243-0565
(615) 741-2241

TEXAS Insurance Commission
P.O. Box 149104
Austin, TX 78714-9104
(512) 463-6464

UTAH Insurance Department
Room 3110
State Office Building
Salt Lake City, UT 84114
(801) 538-3800

VERMONT Insurance Department
89 Main Street
Drawer 20
Montpelier, VT 05620-3101
(802) 828-3301

VIRGINIA Insurance Commission
P.O. Box 1157
Richmond, VA 23209
(804) 371-9741

WASHINGTON Insurance
 Commission
Insurance Building, AQ21
Olympia, WA 98504
(206) 753-7301; (800) 562-6900

WEST VIRGINIA Insurance
 Commission
2019 Washington Street East
Charleston, WV 25305
(304) 558-3394

WISCONSIN Insurance Commission
P.O. Box 7873
Madison, WI 53707-7873
(608) 266-0102

WYOMING Insurance Department
Herschler Building
122 W. 25th Street
Cheyenne, WY 82001
(307) 777-7401

GLOSSARY: UNDERSTANDING THE TERMS

Accidental-death benefit: The provision in a life insurance policy that doubles the face value of the policy if the insured dies in an accident. This is often called double indemnity.

Beneficiary: The person (or the trust fund) named in the policy to receive the benefits of an insurance policy.

Cash surrender value: The amount the insurance company will pay if the policyholder cancels and surrenders the whole-life policy and asks for his or her cash back.

Convertible term insurance: Term insurance that allows the policyholder to change or convert to a cash-value policy without presenting evidence of insurability.

Face amount: The amount stated on the face of the policy; the amount that will be paid at death or maturity of the policy. This figure doesn't include additional payments, such as an accidental-death benefit.

Guaranteed insurability: An option in a life insurance policy that enables a policyholder to buy additional insurance at specified times stated in the policy, say before age 40, without providing evidence of insurability.

Policy loan: The amount that can be borrowed, at a specified rate of interest, from the company by the policyholder. The cash value of the policy is used as collateral for the loan.

Term insurance: Insurance that pays a death benefit if the policyholder dies during a specified period. Term insurance has no cash value.

CHAPTER 5

GREAT EXPECTATIONS

The Financial Side of Preparing for Your Baby's Birth

NUTS AND BOLTS

Starting a family means it's time to start living within your means. Having children is a pricey proposition; it's best to begin to work out a budget before baby makes three.

First, you need to figure out how much money you're going to need to cover your hospital bills. To estimate your out-of-pocket expenses, contact your health insurance company and find out how much you'll have to pay. Most policies require that you pay a deductible of anywhere from several hundred to several thousand dollars, then pay some percentage of your bill after that, up to an established cap. For example, you might have to pay the first $500, then 20 percent of your bill, up to a cap of $5,000. These limits apply to annual medical expenses, so you could easily end up paying the deductible twice if you conceived your child and incurred medical bills during one year but gave birth to the child the following calendar year.

If you don't have enough cash on hand to cover your anticipated expenses, begin saving as soon as possible. In general, health-care practitioners will ask you to pay your share of the bill (the part not covered by health insurance) by the seventh or eighth month of your pregnancy. Talk to your health-care professional, as well as the hospital or birthing center, about payment options; many will work with you to come up with a reasonable payment plan.

It's impossible to anticipate the actual costs of your baby's birth because it's impossible to know what the birth experience will be like for you. Some parents prefer a high-tech birth, one where fetal monitors and painkilling drugs are readily available. Others opt for a low-tech delivery in which understanding women provide comfort and support, and drugs and medical interventions are kept to a minimum. Of course, parents who plan on having a drug-free birth with minimal intervention sometimes wind up having cesarean sections, but two initial decisions—who will assist with the birth and where you will deliver the baby—will go a long way toward determining what your baby's birth will be like.

BABIES, BIRTHS, AND BUDGETS

Starting a family is often all it takes for even the most committed spendthrifts to discover frugality. Raising children is expensive, and for many families the only way to make ends meet is to plan ahead, prepare a family budget, and then stick to it.

Budgeting is the cornerstone of personal financial planning: it helps you understand where your money goes every month, and it helps you set aside funds to meet long-term savings goals. Since many families can't afford to pay for private school, orthodontia, summer camp, and other big-ticket items out of the monthly coffers, advance planning—and saving—is required. Budgeting can become especially important when the family finances are strained because of income lost when one parent stops working to stay at home with the baby or when child-care expenses are added to the budget.

Step 1: Figure Out Where Your Money Is Going

Write down all your family's sources of income on a monthly basis. Then list your monthly expenses: common budgeting categories include housing, food, clothes and shoes, household operation, furniture and household equipment, autos and parts, gas and oil, transportation services, medical expenses, personal business services (lawyers, accountants, banking fees), nondurables (newspapers, toiletries), gifts, and entertainment.

Step 2: Set Your Goals

What are you saving for? College (see Chapter 9)? A family vacation? Tuition for two weeks of summer camp? You might want to divide these into short-term goals (things you want to do this year), medium-term goals (things you want to do in the next five years), and long-term goals (things you want to do in more than five years).

Step 3: Plug in the Numbers

Now it's time to allocate the money to different expense categories. You'll want to look at how much you spent last year and how much you plan to spend this year for the expenses in each category of your budget.

As you prepare your monthly budget, you'll probably want to refer to a book specifically dedicated to personal finance, but the chart beginning on page 88 might help you get started.

WHERE YOU LIVE AND HOW MUCH YOU PAY

As the chart below shows, the cost of having a baby varies widely with region of the country, as well as whether your baby is born vaginally or surgically. Physicians' fees include prenatal and delivery charges.

Location	Cost of Vaginal Delivery	Cost of Cesarean Delivery
Northeast	*$4,848*	*$8,572*
Hospital charges	$3,225	$6,334
Physicians' fees	$1,623	$2,234
Midwest	*$4,514*	*$7,334*
Hospital charges	$2,891	$5,101
Physicians' fees	$1,623	$2,234
South	*$4,561*	*$7,689*
Hospital charges	$2,943	$5,462
Physicians' fees	$1,619	$2,228
West	*$4,640*	*$8,307*
Hospital charges	$3,006	$6,059
Physicians' fees	$1,634	$2,248

SOURCE: Health Insurance Association of America, "Source Book of Health Insurance Data 1992"

Budget for the Month of _____

Expense	Same Month Last Year Amount	Budgeted Amount This Month	Actual Expense
Housing			
rent or mortgage			
real estate taxes			
homeowner's insurance			
water			
heat			
electricity			
gas			
telephone			
Food			
groceries			
eating out			
alcohol			
Clothing and Shoes			
parent 1			
parent 2			
child			
Household Operations			
laundry			
dry cleaning			
repair			

Budget for the Month of _____

Expense	Same Month Last Year Amount	Budgeted Amount This Month	Actual Expense
housekeeping			
gardening			
Medical			
doctor			
dentist			
prescriptions			
over-the-counter drugs			
insurance payments			
Child care			
day care			
baby-sitters			
Child supplies			
toys and games			
lessons and instruction			
diapers			
extracurricular school fees			
sporting goods			
Auto			
loan payments			
insurance			
maintenance			
repair			

Budget for the Month of

Expense	Same Month Last Year Amount	Budgeted Amount This Month	Actual Expense
Gas and Oil			
Household equipment			
furniture			
appliances			
tools			
Transportation			
taxi			
carpool			
parking			
Personal Business			
lawyer			
accountant			
banking fees			
Discretionary Expenses			
newspapers			
magazines			
organization dues			
toiletries			
hobby supplies			
music			
books			
other			

Budget for the Month of _____

Expense	Same Month Last Year Amount	Budgeted Amount This Month	Actual Expense
Entertainment			
movies			
travel			
Gifts			
Misc.			
parent 1			
parent 2			
child			

DOCTOR OR MIDWIFE?

More than any other single factor, the medical professional you choose to assist with the birth will determine what childbirth will be like for you and your partner. Though there are tremendous differences in philosophy and style, your basic choices include an obstetrician, a family practitioner, and a certified nurse-midwife.

If your pregnancy is uncomplicated—and an estimated 70 to 90 percent of pregnancies are—then you could choose a certified nurse-midwife. If you're having a high-risk pregnancy, due to multiple births or any of a number of possible health problems, then you'll probably want to choose a medical doctor. In fact, depending on state licensing laws for midwives, you may have to do so.

As you might imagine, medical doctors tend to use more technology and interventions—and they cost more, too. A 1989 survey by the Health Insurance Association of America found physicians' fees for a normal pregnancy to be about $1,500 and those of a midwife about $1,000. High-risk pregnancies don't necessarily cost more than routine pregnancies unless they result in surgical deliveries, which include higher doctor's fees, operating-room expenses, and scores of incidental add-ons that follow major surgery (see chart on page 87).

Obstetricians handle most of the maternity care in the United States. All licensed obstetricians are medical doctors who have three or more years of specialty training in obstetrics and gynecology. Some have gone on to earn board certification by the American College of Obstetricians and Gynecologists; others may say they are "board eligible," meaning they have completed the training but not passed the ACOG test. Keep in mind that a doctor can call himself or herself a "specialist" without being board certified or keeping up with the requirements of continuing education. To verify that a doctor is board certified, contact the American Board of Medical Specialties or the American Board of Obstetrics and Gynecology (see listings in the Resources section).

Don't assume that an obstetrician who is well versed in the use of technological interventions will always support high-tech births. Some do, but others encourage unmedicated, so-called natural childbirth. You'll have to get references and interview physicians to determine whether you agree on a particular philosophy about childbirth.

Family practitioners are relatively new to the scene. Family practitioners are medical doctors who focus on the total health care of the individual and the family. They also have three years of training following medical school, including at least three months of obstetrics and gynecology. Again, family practice physicians can call themselves specialists without being board certified. To verify a doctor's credentials, contact the American Board of Medical Specialties or the American Board of Family Practice (see listings in the Resources section). Most family practitioners charge more or less the same as an obstetrician for delivering a baby.

Certified nurse-midwives specialize in the care of healthy women with low-risk pregnancies, working with backup physicians who are on-call to consult or take over in case of emergency or complications.

The word midwife comes from the Old English for "with woman." Certified nurse-midwives take a supportive approach to labor and delivery and tend to emphasize childbirth preparation and education and minimize the use of high-tech equipment. They deliver babies in hospitals, birthing centers, and at the parents' home.

The nation's more than 4,200 certified nurse-midwives are registered nurses who have also completed a year or more of training at one of the nearly 40 midwifery programs accredited by the American College of Nurse-Midwives and passed board examinations issued by the ACNM. Almost all states require that midwives pass these hurdles in order to be licensed by the state.

Though midwives deliver more than 80 percent of babies worldwide, they deliver only about 4 percent of the babies in the U.S. That number is growing, however. According to a study by the National Center for Health Statistics, births attended by certified nurse-midwives in hospitals increased from 19,686 in 1975 to 139,229 in 1990, the latest year for which the records were available.

Certified nurse-midwives don't provide second-class medical care. A 1986 U.S. Office of Technology Assessment study determined that care provided by certified nurse-midwives is equivalent to a physician's care and that midwives are better than physicians at providing services requiring communication and preventive action. Also, reports by the National Institute of Medicine and the National Commission to Prevent Infant Mortality praise the contributions of certified nurse-midwives in reducing the incidence of low-birth-weight babies.

Certified nurse-midwives can legally practice in every state, but lay midwives cannot. **Lay midwives** aren't nurses: they have learned to deliver babies through self-study, apprenticeship, and experience. Some states license lay midwives and permit them to deliver babies legally; others have laws classifying them as felons for the "illegal practice of medicine."

If a lay midwife is not licensed, it is difficult to determine if she meets the necessary professional standards. To verify the credentials of certified nurse-midwives, contact the American College of Nurse-Midwives (see listing in the Resources section).

PICKING THE RIGHT HEALTH PROFESSIONAL

Once you've decided which kind of practitioner you want to have assist with your baby's birth, you need to check out the credentials and reputation of your possible candidates. The following steps can help you narrow your list and pick the best health-care professional:

■ Collect at least three recommendations from a number of sources, including your current doctor, friends, family, and city and county medical societies.

■ Check out the educational background of each prospective doctor or midwife. Don't be overawed by educational credentials: doctors and nurses who graduate from prestigious schools have demonstrated academic qualifications, but that is no guarantee of good bedside manner and other skills. If you'll be using a group practice, check the credentials of all members of the group.

■ If you choose a medical doctor, look for one who is board certified. Board certification indicates that a doctor has completed two or four years of residency involving intensive study of a specialty and passed a rigorous exam in the field. A so-called board-eligible doctor has either not taken—or not passed—the specialty board exam. (See Resources section for a list of professional organizations that can verify a doctor's credentials.)

■ If you choose a midwife, look for one who is certified by the American College of Nurse-Midwives. (See Resources section for phone number and address.)

■ Find out whether the doctor or midwife you are considering has been disciplined for medical malpractice. Contact your state medical licensing agency and ask if the doctor has had any actions taken against him or her. Ask the doctor for a list of the other states where he or she has practiced and check with the boards in those states as well. (See list of medical licensing agencies in the Resources section.)

■ Find out where the doctor has staff privileges. Doctors are allowed to practice only in those hospitals where a committee of doctors has reviewed their credentials and found them competent to practice; to be eligible, a doctor must be board certified and recommended by a physician who already has staff privileges.

■ Interview potential candidates. Don't be intimidated by the thought of interviewing a physician or midwife; it's an important and accepted part of selecting a medical professional. Most doctors don't charge for an initial interview, but ask to make sure there isn't a consultation fee.

Consider asking the following questions:

Prenatal Care and Labor Procedures
- How often will I be seen during my pregnancy?
- Who will be available to answer my questions?
- What tests are standard during normal pregnancy care?
- What is your attitude toward breast feeding?
- When do you feel it is necessary to induce labor?
- What is your C-section rate?
- When will you arrive at the hospital or other facility?
- What procedures do you perform routinely? IVs? Enemas? Fetal monitoring? Episiotomy?
- What is your opinion of natural childbirth?
- At what stage of labor would you use an epidural? An analgesic?

Fees, Payment Terms, and Insurance
- What is your fee? (Many doctors charge a flat free for prenatal visits and delivery, with a surcharge of several hundred or $1,000 or more if the baby is delivered by cesarean section.)
- Does that include lab fees? If not, how much more will that be?

- How much more is a cesarean birth?
- When do you want payment?
- Do I have to pay the entire sum and seek reimbursement from my insurance company, or can I pay only the deductible and co-payment?
- If I have to pay before the birth, what happens if I miscarry?

■ Follow your instincts. It's perfectly all right to make your decision based on "feeling" or "gut reaction" as long as you have done your best to ensure that the doctor you select has the qualifications and skills to provide the care you need.

SELECTING THE RIGHT PLACE TO HAVE YOUR BABY

When it comes to picking the right place to give birth, you must face the chicken-and-egg problem: Your choice of hospital or birthing center is restricted to where your doctor or midwife has privileges, and if you want to give birth at home, you'll need to track down a medical team willing to work in your home. For most parents the choice of medical professional is primary and the choice of facility is secondary.

You want your baby to be born in a place that feels safe and comfortable. Each option—a hospital, a birthing center, or a home—offers a different type of security. A hospital offers the security of technology: most facilities are equipped with monitors and equipment to deal with almost any medical emergency. A home offers the security of familiarity: from an emotional point of view, your home is the ideal site for the family-centered experience of birth. Birthing centers fall somewhere in between, providing a comfortable "homelike" setting—with a lot of medical equipment on hand for emergencies. Many hospitals have taken steps to make their maternity areas much more like birthing centers by creating birthing rooms that include facilities for labor, delivery, and recovery rather than the more traditional arrangement of separate rooms for each function.

In addition to the differences in philosophy, there is a significant difference in final cost between hospital and birthing center deliveries. According to the National Association of Childbearing Centers, vaginal births in birthing centers cost 35 to 47 percent less than vaginal births in hospitals. On average hospitals cost $1,000 more per day than birthing centers, according to the Health Insurance Association of America. In 1989, the most recent year for which data are available, the average cost of having a baby in a freestanding birthing center was $2,111, compared to $3,233 for a one-day hospital stay, $4,334 for a two-day hospital stay, or $7,186 for a three-day cesarean-section delivery. The cost of a home birth usually ranges from $800 to $2,000.

As recently as 50 years ago the majority of Americans were born at home. But times change: by 1970, 99.4 percent of births took place in hospitals. Today parents have several options to choose from, each with its distinct advantages:

The hospital delivery room is the safest alternative if there is any possibility that your delivery will have complications. In the past 15 to 20 years hospitals have tried to replace the sterile environment of the hospital delivery room with the warmer, more homelike hospital birthing room. The birthing room has the character of a motel room: there is usually a bed, a rocking chair, a private bath with a shower, a television set, pictures on the walls, and other comforts of home. Most parents prefer this more relaxed decor to the antiseptic, cold atmosphere of the traditional maternity ward. In many cases labor, delivery, and recovery all take place in the same room.

Before deciding where to have your baby, visit any hospital of interest. Consider interviewing a representative of the hospital and asking the following:

❑ What percentage of women give birth via cesarean sections?
❑ How often is epidural anesthesia used during birth?
❑ What percentage of women have IVs? Enemas? Shaving? Episiotomies?
❑ Is rooming-in permitted? (i.e., can my baby stay with me rather than being kept in a nursery?)
❑ Can my other children visit?
❑ What childbirth preparation methods do the staff members know?
❑ What childbirth classes are offered?
❑ Can the baby's father attend the birth? What about another coach or support person?

- ❑ Can the baby's father witness the birth if a cesarean section is required?
- ❑ If there are no complications, can Mom breast-feed the baby immediately after the birth?
- ❑ Is an early leave possible?

THE PATIENT'S BILL OF RIGHTS

This Patient's Bill of Rights has been prepared by the American Hospital Association:

1. **The patient has the right to considerate and respectful care.**

2. **The patient has the right to obtain from his or her physician complete current information concerning his or her diagnosis, treatment, and prognosis** in terms the patient can be reasonably expected to understand. When it is not medically advisable to give such information to the patient, the information should be made available to an appropriate person on his or her behalf. He or she has the right to know, by name, the physician responsible for coordinating his or her care.

3. **The patient has the right to receive from his or her physician information necessary to give informed consent prior to the start of any procedure and/or treatment.** Except in emergencies, such information for informed consent should include but not necessarily be limited to the specific procedure and/or treatment, the medically significant risks involved, and the probable duration of incapacitation. Where medically significant alternatives for care or treatment exist or when the patient requests information concerning medical alternatives, the patient has the right to such information. The patient also has the right to know the name of the person responsible for the procedures and/or treatment.

4. **The patient has the right to refuse treatment** to the extent permitted by law and to be informed of the medical consequences of his or her action.

5. **The patient has the right to every consideration of his or her privacy** concerning his or her own medical-care program. Case discussion, consultation, examination, and treatment are confidential and should be conducted discreetly. Those not directly involved in the patient's care must have his or her permission to be present.

6. **The patient has the right to expect that all communications and records pertaining to his or her care should be treated as confidential.**

7. **The patient has the right to expect that within its capacity, a hospital must make reasonable response to the request of a patient for services**. The hospital must provide evaluation, service, and/or referral as indicated by the urgency of the case. When medically permissible, a patient must be transferred to another facility only after he or she has received complete information and explanation concerning the need for an alternative to such a transfer. The institution to which the patient is to be transferred must first have accepted the patient for transfer.

8. **The patient has the right to obtain information as to any relationship of his or her hospital to other health-care and educational institutions** insofar as his or her care is concerned. The patient has the right to obtain information as to the existence of any professional relationships among individuals, by name, who are treating him or her.

9. **The patient has the right to be advised if the hospital proposes to engage in or perform human experimentation** affecting his or her care or treatment. The patient has the right to refuse to participate in such research projects.

10. **The patient has the right to expect reasonable continuity of care**. He or she has the right to know in advance what appointment times and physicians are available and where. The patient has the right to expect that the hospital will provide a mechanism whereby he or she is informed by his or her physician or a delegate of the physician of the patient's continuing health-care requirements following discharge.

11. **The patient has the right to examine and receive an explanation of his or her bill**, regardless of source of payment.

12. **The patient has the right to know what hospital rules and regulations apply to his or her conduct as a patient.**

Birthing centers are very much like hospital birthing rooms, except they are usually not attached to hospitals. At the nearly 130 birthing centers around the country, babies are usually delivered by midwives under the supervision of an obstetrician on 24-hour call.

For low-risk births the biggest difference between a birthing center and a hospital birthing room is the cost. According to the National Association of Childbearing Centers, the fee can be one-half to two-thirds the cost of a hospital stay. One reason for the lower bills is that the centers encourage one-day stays. In some cases you can bring your baby home hours after the birth.

As might be expected, birthing centers tend to have a lower rate of cesarean sections: the cesarean section rate for women in birthing centers averages about half the rate for low-risk births in hospitals. A study published in the *New England Journal of Medicine* in 1989 showed that women who chose birthing centers had about the same rate of problem-free deliveries as women who gave birth in hospitals. In general, women who deliver in birthing centers are subject to fewer medical interventions, such as IVs, electronic fetal monitoring, episiotomies, forceps, analgesia, and anesthesia.

Most birthing centers aren't equipped to deal with emergencies. However, all are affiliated with nearby hospitals, and some are actually physically attached to hospitals. Of course, problems do occasionally arise. About 3 out of 10 first-time mothers have to be transferred to a hospital from a birthing center because of prolonged labor or complications, according to the study in the *New England Journal of Medicine*. The rate drops to 1 out of 10 for women who have already had a baby.

If you object to the "medicalization" of childbirth and want to minimize the use of high-tech equipment and drugs, consider a birthing center. Check with your medical professional first to make sure that there are no risk factors indicating that you should be in a hospital.

To find a birthing center staffed by a certified nurse-midwife and accredited by the Commission for the Accreditation of Freestanding Birth Centers, contact the National Association of Childbearing Centers, 3123 Gottschall Road, Perkiomenville, PA 18074-9546; (215) 234-8068, (215) 234-0564.

When you visit a birthing center, ask a representative the following questions:

- Does the birthing center operate within a hospital?
- If not, which hospital is the center affiliated with?
- What are the procedures for transferring a patient from the center to the hospital? What is the protocol in case of emergency?
- Does the center provide prenatal, childbirth, and postpartum care and education?
- What emergency equipment is on hand?
- Is primary care provided by certified nurse-midwives?
- What kind of physician backup is available?

- What childbirth preparation methods are used?
- What childbirth classes does the facility offer?
- Who can attend the birth?
- How long can Mom and baby stay?

In your grandparents' day almost all babies were born at home; today, almost all babies are born away from home. But in recent years there has been something of a revival of home birth under the watchful eye of an experienced midwife.

Home births are the least expensive alternative, often one-half to one-third the cost of a birth in a birthing center or hospital. But home birth should be considered only if your pregnancy is low risk and there are no signs of complications.

Most home births are tended by certified nurse-midwives or lay midwives. For additional information contact the Association for Childbirth at Home; Informed Homebirth/Informed Birth & Parenting; National Association of Parents and Professionals for Safe Alternatives in Childbirth; and the Center for Humane Options in Childbirth Experience (listed in the Resources section).

STUDYING FOR THE BIG DAY

Whether your baby is born in a state-of-the-art hospital or in your bedroom at home, childbirth education classes can help to prepare you for the experience. Childbirth is much more participatory than it was a generation or two ago: women are no longer rendered unconscious during the delivery, and fathers are no longer restricted to waiting rooms.

The first childbirth education classes were known as "natural childbirth" classes, and they were designed to help women overcome their fear—and their need for medication—by explaining the birth process to them. Today some classes still focus on ways to go "natural" and avoid drugs, but the majority involve education about the entire range of possibilities during labor and delivery. Learning relaxation techniques and breathing are part of most programs.

Childbirth classes give couples a chance to get their questions answered, to share their experiences with other expectant couples, to practice their coping strategies, and to teach the coaches about ways they can be most supportive of their partners.

There are a number of different philosophies on childbirth education, though many instructors include bits and pieces of other approaches. For help comparing different childbirth education methods and to find out what classes are available in your area, call the International Childbirth Education Association at (612) 854-8660.

LET THEM KNOW YOU'RE COMING

You can save yourself time and trouble—and in some cases money—by notifying the hospital or birthing center and your insurance company of the impending birth before your baby arrives. If the hospital or birthing center permits, preregister by filling out the paperwork in advance. With the administrative details out of the way, you won't have to deal with the pain of filling out forms in triplicate on top of labor pains.

With many insurance companies you need to notify the company and get a precertification number in order to receive full coverage for your expenses. The time frame for doing so may be different from the one that governs most hospital stays, so be sure to check. In many cases your insurer will issue you a precertification number for use on all your bills and for paperwork related to the birth. If you fail to precertify, many insurance companies will charge an additional fee or refuse to pay a percentage of your benefits.

ISSUES TO DISCUSS:
WHAT PARENTS SHOULD TALK ABOUT

- ❏ Who will assist with the birth? An obstetrician? A family practitioner? A midwife?
- ❏ Where do we want our child to be born? A hospital? A birthing center? At home?
- ❏ Whom would we like to be present at the birth? Will the facility we choose allow these people to be present?
- ❏ Who will review with the insurance company exactly what expenses will be covered?

- How much will our out-of-pocket expenses be?
- Do we have enough cash available to cover our share of the medical bill for the baby's birth?
- Have we established a budget to meet our financial obligations in regard to our addition to the family?
- Who will be responsible for filing the preregistration forms with the hospital or birth facility?
- Who will be responsible for obtaining precertification from the insurance company?

ON LEAVE: YOUR MATERNITY AND PATERNITY RIGHTS

After nearly eight years of congressional debate the Family Medical Leave Act became law in 1993. At its most basic level the law requires businesses with 50 or more employees to provide up to 12 weeks a year of unpaid, job-protected leave to eligible employees, male or female. Sanctioned reasons for leave include the birth or adoption of a child, as well as the care of a child, spouse, or parent with a serious health condition.

To be eligible, the employee must have been employed for at least one year. After the leave the employee must be restored to his or her former position or to "an equivalent position" with the same benefits and pay as the job before the leave.

While Congress was wrangling over the bill, more than half the states went ahead and passed their own versions of family and medical leave legislation. Of course, in states where the state law is more generous than the federal law, the state law applies.

In addition Mom may be guaranteed a certain amount of paid maternity leave by federal law. The Pregnancy Discrimination Act, a 1978 amendment to Title VII of the Civil Rights Act of 1964, states that discrimination on the basis of pregnancy, childbirth, or related medical conditions constitutes unlawful sex discrimination.

This law says that an employer with more than 15 people on the payroll must treat pregnancy as if it were a medical disability. A woman giving birth must get the same amount of paid leave as employees who cannot work because of illness or injury, usually six to eight weeks. In addition she must be guaranteed that she will get her job back at the same salary. If the company doesn't provide leave to anyone for temporary medical conditions, then no special case needs to be made for pregnancy and childbirth.

For additional information on the Pregnancy Discrimination Act call the Equal Employment Opportunity Commission at (800) 669-3362.

QUESTIONS & ANSWERS

Should I choose a private or semiprivate room?

It depends on how much privacy you can afford. Obviously private rooms cost more—check with your hospital to find out how much more—but many women find the quiet well worth the additional cost, especially if the hospital allows rooming-in. Many insurance companies pay only for a semiprivate room but allow their patients to stay in the more expensive private room if they agree to pay the difference between the room rates.

My doctor is board certified. How can I find out what that really means?

You're smart to be skeptical of claims that a doctor is board certified. Indeed, not all medical boards are alike. Any group of physicians can set up a specialty board, but they don't necessarily have to establish meaningful standards. Of the approximately 150 different medical boards in existence the American Board of Medical Specialties has certified only 23 as meeting its standards.

To find out if your doctor is certified by a particular board, contact the American Board of Medical Specialties, 47 Perimeter Center East, Suite 500, Atlanta, GA 30346, (800) 776-2378.

Note that most board-certified doctors become members of their medical specialty societies; doctors who meet the full requirements for membership are called "fellows" of the society. For instance, the title "FACOG" following a physician's name indicates that the doctor is also a Fellow of the American College of Obstetricians and Gynecologists.

Are there any requirements that my doctor stay current with the latest technological developments?

Amazingly, no. Once a physician has been licensed, he or she can continue to practice medicine without ever being recertified by demonstrating knowledge or competence. Doctors do need to keep their medical licenses renewed, but they need only attend a certain minimum number of continuing education classes; no demonstration of skills is needed to keep a medical license in force.

I have learned that some insurance companies won't pay for the baby to stay in the hospital if the mother has a medical complication and needs to stay in the hospital an extra day or two after the birth. Do insurance companies require some babies to go home without their mothers?

Yes, some insurance companies will discharge the baby without the mother in the name of cost savings. It's up to the doctor and the hospital to determine the length of your stay. If absolutely necessary, you could pay the bill yourself. Check with your insurance company before the birth and ask under what conditions your baby could be discharged without you.

Will my insurance company pay for a midwife?

Most do, but ask to be sure. Nurse-midwife services are covered by most private insurance, Medicare, Medicaid, and managed-care programs. Nurse-midwives are also covered under the Civilian Health and Medical Program of the Uniformed Services and Federal Employees Health Plans. Ask your insurer what will happen if complications arise and your baby is delivered by cesarean section. Some insurance companies will pay for either a certified nurse-midwife or an obstetrician, but not both.

I just learned that I have placenta previa, and I will be on bed rest for the next three months. Will I qualify for disability insurance?

Probably, but it depends on your policy. Some disability insurance policies cover maternity complications; others do not. For additional information on disability insurance see Chapter 4.

Due to a rise in my blood pressure late in my pregnancy, my doctor has scheduled a cesarean delivery. Will my insurance company pay for it?

Yes. As long as the procedure is performed for sound medical reasons, your insurance company should cover both scheduled and emergency C-sections. It's best to notify your insurance company of the date and reason for the procedure so that you can get all the necessary precertification out of the way before you head for the hospital.

STEP BY STEP:
PREPARING FOR THE BABY'S BIRTH

- ❑ Estimate your out-of-pocket expenses.
- ❑ Prepare a budget, including the expenses associated with your child's birth and first days at home.
- ❑ Get recommendations for doctors and midwives.
- ❑ Check credentials.
- ❑ Interview prospective doctors and midwives.
- ❑ Pick a medical processional.
- ❑ Visit various hospitals, birthing centers, and other alternatives.
- ❑ Register for childbirth classes.
- ❑ Attend childbirth classes.
- ❑ Review insurance coverage.
- ❑ Estimate total out-of-pocket costs.
- ❑ Preregister with the hospital.
- ❑ Follow the insurance company's precertification procedures.

ARE YOU COVERED? QUESTIONS TO ASK YOUR INSURANCE COMPANY

As soon as you find out you are pregnant—if not before—check with your insurance company to confirm your exact maternity benefits. Don't assume a procedure is covered simply because your doctor says it is routine. Questions to ask your insurer:

- ❑ What specific benefits are covered?
    - – Prenatal care?
    - – Prenatal tests?
    - – Routine sonograms? How many?
    - – Prenatal hospitalization?
    - – Vitamins?
    - – Amniocentesis?
    - – Chorionic villus sampling (CVS)?
    - – Genetic testing?
    - – Delivery at a birthing center? At home?
    - – C-section?
    - – Services of a certified nurse-midwife? Is the midwife covered if a physician is called in to deliver the baby due to complications?

- How many hospital days are covered with a vaginal delivery?
- How many hospital days are covered with a cesarean delivery?
- I am hospitalized for a medical problem after delivery, will the insurance company pay for my baby to stay with me? For how long?

❏ What are the deductibles and co-payments?
- What will my estimated out-of-pocket costs be?
- Are there any limits or caps on maternity care?

❏ What are the benefits for the baby?
- Is my baby's care covered by my individual insurance policy? For how long?
- What if the baby has to be in the intensive-care nursery?
- If my baby needs to have home monitoring, oxygen therapy, or other special treatments at home, will the insurance company pay? For how long?
- Will circumcision be covered?
- Is hospital nursery care covered?
- Is well-baby care covered?
- Will the policy cover visits from pediatricians not in my plan who may be called in?

If possible, make sure you are insured during the entire term of pregnancy. Babies don't always respect schedules; they can arrive early—before the insurance coverage is in force.

When you call to clarify your benefits, get the name of the person you spoke with. Ask for a letter confirming your maternity benefits. If the insurer won't send a letter, write your own letter outlining the benefits you expect to receive, as confirmed by the person you spoke to on the phone. Tell the company in your letter that you will assume the coverage is correct as written, unless you hear back from the company within 10 business days. Such a letter wouldn't be legally binding in a dispute, but it could give you an edge in a battle over whether or not certain benefits should be paid for.

RESOURCES:
WHERE TO GO FOR MORE INFORMATION

BOOKS

■ **Having Your Baby with a Nurse-Midwife**, by the American College of Nurse-Midwives and Sandra Jacobs. Cost: $9.95, plus $1.50 shipping and handling. Contact: Little, Brown & Company, Attention: Order Department, 200 West Street, Watham, MA 02254; (800) 759-0190, (212) 633-4400.

■ **Homebirth**, by Sheila Kitzinger. Cost: $18.95 (hardback), plus $2.50 shipping and handling. Contact: Houghton Mifflin, Attention: Customer Service, Wayside Road, Burlington, MA 01803; (800) 225-3362, (212) 213-4800

■ **Take This Book to the Obstetrician with You: A Consumer's Guide to Pregnancy and Childbirth**, by Karla Morales and Charles Inlander. Cost: $9.95, plus $3 shipping and handling. Contact: Addison-Wesley Publishing Co., (617) 944-3700.

■ **The Midwife Challenge**, edited by Sheila Kitzinger. Cost: $12.95, plus $2.75 shipping and handling. Contact: Pandora Press, P.O. Box 588, Dunmore, PA 18512; (800) 242-7737, (212) 207-7000.

■ **100 Ways to Be a Savvy Medical Consumer**, by the People's Medical Society. Cost: $5.95. Contact: People's Medical Society, 462 Walnut Street, Allentown, PA 18102; (215) 770-1670.

■ **The Consumer's Legal Guide to Today's Health Care**, by Stephen Isaacs and Ava Swartz. Cost: $12.95, plus $2.50 shipping and handling. Contact: Houghton Mifflin, Attention: Customer Service, Wayside Road, Burlington, MA 01803; (800) 225-3362, (212) 213-4800.

BROCHURES AND PAMPHLETS

■ "The Patient's Bill of Rights," by the American Hospital Association. Cost: Free. Contact: American Hospital Association, Attention: Resource Center, 840 North Lake Shore Drive, Chicago, IL 60611; (800) 242-2626, (312) 280-6000.

■ "Today's Certified Nurse-Midwife," by the American College of Nurse-Midwives. Cost: Free. Contact: American College of Nurse-Midwives, 818 Connecticut Ave. NW, Suite 900, Washington, DC 20006; (202) 289-0171.

■ "Is Home Birth for You?" and "Working with a Birth Assistant," by Informed Homebirth/Informed Birth & Parenting. Cost: Free. Contact: Informed Homebirth/Informed Birth & Parenting, P.O. Box 3675, Ann Arbor, MI 48106; (313) 662-6857.

■ "Which Medical Specialist for You?" by the American Board of Medical Specialties. Cost: $1.50. Contact: American Board of Medical Specialties, 1007 Church Street, Suite 404, Evanston, IL 60201-5913; (800) 776-2378, (708) 491-9091.

■ "Helping You Choose: Quality Hospital Care," by the Joint Commission on Accreditation of Health Care Organization. Cost: Free. Contact: Joint Commission on Accreditation of Health Care Organizations, Customer Service Department, One Renaissance Boulevard, Oakbrook Terrace, IL 60181; (708) 916-5600.

■ "The Birth Center: Safe and Sensitive Care," by the National Association of Childbearing Centers. Cost: $1. Contact: National Association of Childbearing Centers, 3123 Gottschall Road, Perkiomenville, PA 18074; (215) 234-8068.

ORGANIZATIONS

- **American Board of Family Practice**, 2228 Young Drive, Lexington, KY 40505; (606) 269-5626.

- **American Board of Medical Specialties**, 1007 Church Street, Suite 404, Evanston, IL 60201-5913; (800) 776-2378, (708) 491-9091.

- **American Board of Obstetrics and Gynecology**, 2915 Vine Street, Dallas, TX 75204; (214) 871-1619.

- **American College of Nurse-Midwives**, 818 Connnecticut Ave. NW, Suite 900, Washington, DC 20006; (202) 289-0171.

- **American College of Obstetricians and Gynecologists**, 409 12th Street SW, Washington, DC 20024-2188; (202) 638-5577.

- **American Hospital Association**, 840 North Lake Shore Drive, Chicago, IL 60611; (312) 280-6000.

- **American Osteopathic Association**, 142 East Ontario Street, Chicago, IL 60611; (800) 621-1773.

- **Association for Childbirth at Home, International**, Glendale Birth Center, 116 South Lowing, Glendale, CA 91205; (213) 663-4996.

- **Center for Humane Options in Childbirth Experience**, 3474 North High Street, Columbus, OH 43214; (614) 263-2229.

- **Health Insurance Association of America**, 1025 Connecticut Avenue NW, Washington, DC 20036-3998; (202) 223-7782.

- **Informed Homebirth/Informed Birth & Parenting**, P.O. Box 3675, Ann Arbor, MI 48106; (313) 662-6857.

- **Joint Commission on Accreditation of Health Care Organizations**, One Renaissance Boulevard, Oakbrook Terrace, IL 60181; (708) 916-5600.

- **Midwives Alliance of North America**, P.O. Box 175, Newton, KS 67114; (316) 283-4543.

- **National Association of Childbearing Centers**, 3123 Gottschall Road, Perkiomenville, PA 18074-9546; (215) 234-8068.

- **National Association of Parents & Professionals for Safe Alternatives in Childbirth**, Route 1, Box 646, Marble Hill, MO 63764; (314) 238-2010.

- **People's Medical Society**, 462 Walnut Street, Allentown, PA 18102; (215) 770-1670; (800) 624-8773.

CHAPTER 6

SPECIAL DELIVERY

Getting the Most for Your Medical Dollar

NUTS AND BOLTS

Now that the baby has arrived, you can be sure that the bills will follow. Don't expect one single neat, itemized bill from the hospital or birthing center and another, equally neat, from your doctor or midwife. Instead look for a series of bills—from the hospital or birthing center, the pharmacy, doctors, anesthesiologists, pediatricians, and even other health professionals you may not have heard of or met. In many cases different bills will have different deductibles and co-payments, depending on whether certain physicians or treatments are covered under your health-care plan.

Though the bills will trickle in from a number of sources, the average hospital bill in 1991 totaled $4,720 for a vaginal delivery and $7,826 for a cesarean section—more in metropolitan areas and the Northeast. The cost of having a baby has reached these astronomical heights despite the fact that the length of time spent in the hospital has dropped dramatically. In the 1950s women used to stay in the hospital for 12 to 14 days after giving birth. The length of the stays gradually dropped to about five days by the 1970s, but today many new mothers are home one day after meeting their baby face to face for the first time.

Do yourself a favor: Estimate your total health-care costs and your out-of-pocket costs *before* the onset of labor. This should help you design a health-care record-keeping system that will assist you in filing claims and seeking reimbursement. That may also be helpful come tax time, as you may need the figures if you qualify for an itemized tax deduction for medical expenses.

Keeping good records of your medical treatment is the cornerstone of managing your health-care spending. Most health insurance companies do not cover everything. Each year they expect you to pay a certain basic fee, called the deductible, before they will cover any bills. Thereafter they expect you to cover a certain percentage of the allowable bill—the co-payment. For example, if your policy has a $250 deductible and a 20 percent co-pay, each year you pay the first $250 and 20 percent of the total bill after that. That's why you can save yourself—and your insurance company—some money by keeping detailed records and double-checking your bill.

Mother really does know best—at least when it comes to assessing whether a certain medical service or treatment was performed. The problem is, in the weeks (or months) between the time the baby is delivered and the bills are delivered, enough time has passed that few mothers can remember exactly what happened to them in the hospital. To avoid having to pay the price of forgetfulness, write it all down in a daily diary of events. The work sheets on pages 121 through 123 may provide a good guide.

When you and your baby leave the hospital, request an itemized bill. If a detailed bill isn't available when it's time to check out of the hospital, ask to have one mailed to you. (Many facilities won't provide an itemized bill unless you ask for one, especially if your insurance company pays them directly.) Ask for a bill that lists the charges in English; otherwise, you're likely to get only a long list of undecipherable computer codes. You have a right to understand what you are being asked to pay for.

When the bill arrives, carefully scrutinize it for errors. Unfortunately the odds are excellent that you'll find at least one mistake, and the larger the bill, the greater the likelihood of error. Carefully check it over for errors.

One reason for the frequency of errors is that most hospitals bill patients for services and supplies before they are delivered. Often the doctor orders a treatment and the bill is processed immediately; if the patient's course of treatment changes or if she is discharged early, the bill may or may not be updated. Billing errors are most common with surgery since there are so many additional services and charges.

Some of the most common billing errors or maternity bills include

- Billing for a private rather than a semiprivate room;
- Billing for an incorrect number of days in the facility;
- Billing for supplies and medications that were not received;
- Billing for nursery care even though the baby stayed in the room;
- Billing for a labor room that wasn't used because of a quick delivery;
- Billing for personal items not received or not allowed to be taken home.

Don't be surprised to receive a separate set of bills in your baby's name. Use the same system of recording treatments and double-checking bills for your baby's health-care bills.

IT PAYS TO COMPLAIN

If you discover a problem with your bill when you review your records, don't assume the error must be yours or that correcting the bill won't be worth the trouble. Errors are common, and a little persistence is certainly worth your while. Start by contacting a representative of the hospital and asking for an explanation of the charges listed on your itemized bill. Explain the problem clearly, and be polite. If the problem is not immediately resolved, follow up by filing a written complaint, noting the name of the person you spoke to.

Still no response? Write again, this time to the administrator of the hospital or birthing center.

If you continue to strike out, it's time to seek help from other authorities. Consider contacting:

- The state medical society or board. These professional associations often have mechanisms to resolve disagreements between health professionals and patients. For a list of state medical boards see the Resources section of this chapter.

- The state health department. Health professionals must be licensed by the state. Many of these licensing boards also handle dispute settlement. For a list of state health departments see the Resources section of this chapter.
- Contact a lawyer. You may be surprised at how quickly a letter on an attorney's letterhead can get results.

STAKE YOUR CLAIM

After you have reviewed the hospital bill, you should file a claim with your insurance company. If your hospital or birthing center "accepts assignment" of benefits, then you'll be billed a rate equal to the "reasonable and customary" charges, an amount the insurance company has deemed fair payment for service. Doctors who don't accept assignment may charge more than the reasonable and customary fee, and you'll have to pay the difference. For example, if your doctor charges $300 for a sonogram but your insurance company considers $250 the reasonable and customary charge, it's up to you to pay your doctor the $50 difference between the portion covered by insurance and the physician's total bill.

Before the paper shuffle begins, set up a filing system. Keep a separate file for Mother and baby and file the claims as soon as possible. If you let the bills pile up, you are more likely to lose or forget them. And if you're expecting to get money back, the longer you wait to submit the claim, the longer the insurance company holds on to the money that rightfully belongs to you.

Make copies of your completed insurance forms for your records before filing any claims. Keep these copies in your filing system and attach the insurance company's response to the bill. Keep copies of all correspondence about the same matter in the same file. Use a master sheet to keep track of the date you file a claim and the date you receive payment. The work sheet on page 123 will help you create a master filing system.

If you have a question about your insurance coverage or about the denial of a claim, call the company. Most have toll-free, 800 numbers. Always keep a record of the date, time, and name of the person you talked to when you called.

These days many families must juggle their claims between mothers' and fathers' insurance companies. As a rule, if two insurance companies are involved, you should first submit the claim to the mother's insurer, which has primary responsibility for it. After the mother's insurance company has paid its share, send it to the father's company to pick up the balance.

Just as you complained about a billing error, raise your voice if you think your insurance company has turned down a claim that you believe is legitimate.

Start by writing a letter to the insurance company, explaining your position and asking for an explanation of the denial of payment in writing. This will probably begin a round of letters back and forth. Protect yourself from charges that a particular letter did not arrive by sending your correspondence by certified mail, return receipt requested. Of course, keep copies of all correspondence and *never* send your original policy. Watch for deadlines to appeal your bill.

If the insurance company fails to handle the matter to your satisfaction, contact your state insurance department. You won't necessarily win the dispute, but the state insurance department will certainly see to it that the company responds to your complaints. In your correspondence with the insurance department enclose copies of your written exchange with the company and once again clearly and rationally explain your position. Include the name of the company and your policy number at the top of your letter. (For a list of state insurance departments see the Resources section of Chapter 4.)

Can't get no satisfaction? Contact a lawyer who is knowledgeable in insurance matters.

IF YOU'RE UNINSURED

An estimated 36 million Americans do not have health insurance and 60 million more are inadequately insured. Some can't afford to buy coverage; others are denied coverage because of a history of illness or disability.

If you can't afford health insurance, contact your state health department and ask for help in contacting free or low-cost clinics in your area. If you can afford to pay but have been denied access to health insurance because you have been sick or disabled, consider joining a group that offers to sell health insurance to its members. The National Organization for Women, as well as many school alumni associations and professional organizations, often makes insurance available to members.

Another option: Contact the state insurance department and ask if any insurance companies in the state offer open enrollment periods. During open enrollment the company will insure anyone—including people with preexisting conditions—though the policy may exclude the preexisting condition for a specified period.

The state insurance department can also tell you about risk-sharing pools, which are now set up in about half the states. The requirements vary from state to state, but generally you must be a resident of the state and have been turned down for insurance by at least one company. If you qualify, you have the right to buy insurance at prices about 25 to 50 percent higher than normal. A dip in the risk-sharing pool won't come cheap, but it may be the only option open to you.

CUTTING COSTS WITHOUT CUTTING CORNERS

Tips on saving on your medical bill:

- **File claims ASAP**. Some insurance policies won't pay claims filed six months after treatment.
- **Follow the rules**. If your insurance company requires precertification before you enter the hospital, then by all means precertify. Unless you go into labor early, you should have plenty of time to notify the insurance company of the impending birth. Since some insurers will penalize you for not following the appropriate procedures, go ahead and get a precertification number well before your anticipated due date. If your insurance company has a specific prescription plan that requires you to use particular pharmacies, be sure you do so to get maximum benefits.
- **Don't wait patiently**. If your insurance company delays reimbursement, complain to the company, then take up the issue with the state insurance department. About half the states require health insurers to pay claims within a specified number of days, typically 30 or 40.

- **Buy generic drugs**. If any painkillers or other prescription drugs are required after you leave the hospital, ask your doctor to prescribe a generic, which may cost up to 50 percent less than a brand-name drug. Check with the pharmacist about substitutes if you forget to have your doctor mark the prescription. In many states the pharmacist is allowed to make the substitution unless the physician marks "dispense as written" on the prescription. Generics may save money both in the checkout line and when it comes time for reimbursement from your insurance company: Many insurers pay 100 percent of the costs of generic drugs but only 80 percent of the cost of name-brand drugs.
- **Don't phone home**. Get some rest and call your friends with the good news when you get home. Or if you do want to chat or talk to close family, use your own telephone calling card rather than billing through the hospital. Phone calls aren't covered by even the most generous insurance plans.
- **Take advantage of flexible spending accounts**. If your employer offers a flexible spending account, use it. Though only about 15 percent of all eligible employees use the account, they can add up to significant health-care savings.

Here's how they work: You estimate your family's annual out-of-pocket health-care expenses, up to the maximum amount established by your employer (usually about $3,000). Your employer deducts the money from your salary over the course of the year and deposits it in a special account where you can draw on it to pay for your out-of-pocket medical expenses, including your deductibles and co-payments.

The advantage to you: The money that is set aside in your flexible spending account is not subject to Social Security or personal income tax. (In many places you're also spared state and local taxes.)

The tax savings can add up fast. A married person with a household income of $50,000 a year who pays $3,000 worth of medical bills from a flexible account would save approximately $1,000 in taxes. Don't assume you can claim the medical expenses as a deduction on your income tax return. You can only deduct that portion that exceeds 7.5 percent of your adjusted gross income—a considerable sum. (See Chapter 8 for additional information.)

The downside: Flexible spending accounts follow the "use it or lose it" system of accounting. Any money in the account not used during the year becomes the property of your employer.

ISSUES TO DISCUSS:
WHAT PARENTS SHOULD TALK ABOUT

- ❑ Who should be responsible for setting up and maintaining our health insurance claims file?
- ❑ What records do we want to keep while mother is in the hospital or birthing center?
- ❑ Who will review the medical bills?
- ❑ Who will submit the bills to the insurance company?
- ❑ Who will be responsible for paying the medical bills not covered by insurance?
- ❑ Have we done everything possible to minimize our costs?

QUESTIONS & ANSWERS

When does a hospital "day" begin and end?

It varies from hospital to hospital. Like hotels, most hospitals have a checkout time before noon. You should be out of bed and out the door or you'll be charged for an extra day.

I am concerned about being released from the hospital before I am ready— or before my baby is. What can I do?

Talk to your doctor. You're right to be concerned—hospital stays are growing shorter. Today the average length hospital stay is one day for a vaginal delivery and three days for a cesarean delivery. Since some problems don't show up until several days after birth, parents have to keep an eye out for jaundice and other complications. Your doctor can put a word in with the insurance company and try to extend your stay if it is justified on medical grounds. If you're concerned about taking care of the baby on your own, consider hiring a practical nurse or mother substitute to help you out for a few weeks after you get home.

Can I pay my bill over time?

Yes. Most medical facilities will allow you to make payments—with interest—on your bill. Contact the accounting department for details, since the policies vary from facility to facility.

I want a copy of my medical records, but my doctor doesn't want to give them to me. What can I do?

It depends on where you live. In the past, medical records were considered the property of the doctor, and patients had almost no right to see or copy them. But times change. Today more than half the states have laws guaranteeing patients access to their medical records. To find out about your state's laws, contact the medical licensing body in your state or call the American Medical Association's Washington, DC, office at (202) 789-7400.

My spouse and I both have insurance. How should we handle our claims?

Depending on the flexibility of your plans, you may be able to arrange things so that you can get virtually all of your health-care costs covered by insurance. First you should decide on one policy as your primary insurer. In making the selection, consider the coverage, deductibles, and co-insurance requirements.

When it comes time to file a claim, you must first submit the claim to your primary insurer. After you have collected from the first company, you can file a claim with the second company, including evidence of what your other policy has already paid. The second policy will "coordinate" benefits so that you cannot make money by collecting more than 100 percent of the bill.

As a rule, if you and your spouse both work outside the home and have insurance supplied by your respective employers, a husband's plan is primary for him and secondary for his spouse, and a wife's plan is primary for her and secondary for her spouse. When the children are covered under both policies, their primary insurer is determined by either the birthday rule (the policy of the parent with the earlier birthday will be the primary insurer) or the gender rule (the husband's policy is primary for the children and the wife's is secondary). If you and your spouse have insurance companies that use different rules for determining coverage for the children, ask the companies how they plan to handle claims for your baby before the baby is born.

When should my child be added to my health insurance policy?

As soon as he or she is born or legally adopted. If your health insurance policy covers the family, your baby should be automatically covered, but it's best to notify the insurance company in advance. (For details see Chapter 3.)

My doctor billed me $100 for a procedure, but my insurance company only credited me with paying $75 toward my deductible. Why?

Your insurance company will calculate your deductible on the basis of the eligible—not the actual—expenses. In this case your insurance company considered $75 the usual, reasonable, and customary fee, so only that amount was credited toward your deductible.

What can I take with me when I leave the hospital?

More than you think. At least when you're leaving the hospital, you often can take it with you when you go. You will have to pay for anything that has been opened or partially used, so you might as well bring it home with you. The take-home list might include disposable diapers, sanitary pads, ointments, foam mattress pads, gauze pads, nursing pads, pacifiers, bottles of formula or water, and other items that cannot be laundered or washed and reused.

My employer offers a "cafeteria-style" benefits package. How do I know what kind of health insurance to choose?

You're going to need to estimate your total costs under each health-care option. You may have your choice of several plans, including a *health maintenance organization* (HMO), in which you pay a monthly fee and a nominal fee—$5 or $10—for each visit, but your choice of doctors and pediatricians is restricted to those participating in the program; a *preferred provider organization*, in which you pay a somewhat higher monthly fee, an annual deductible, and a percentage of your medical bills, and you can see any of the doctors participating in the program (some plans also allow you to get care outside the plan, but you'll have to pay a larger share of the bill); and a *traditional fee-for-service plan*, in which you choose your own doctors and pay a deductible and a percentage of the bill in addition to a monthly premium. (There are a number of variations on these themes, but these are the basics.) To figure out which plan is best for you, you'll have to estimate your total bill—including a probable schedule for doctors' visits—and calculate how much you would pay in premiums, deductibles, and co-payments under each plan option. If you need help, contact your employee benefits office for assistance.

DAILY DIARY: IN THE HOSPITAL

DOCTOR VISITS

Name	Date	What Was Done or Said	Comments

MEDICATION LOG

Date	Time	Drug	Dosage/Form	Dispensed By

DAILY DIARY: IN THE HOSPITAL

SUPPLIES

Date	Item Used	Who Gave It

TELEPHONE LOG

Date	Time	Party You Called	Length of Call

CREATING A MEDICAL-CLAIMS DIARY

THE BILL			**CLAIM**				
Date of Service	**Provider**	**Fee**	**Name Insurer**	**Date Filed**	**Amount Paid**	**Date Paid**	**Paid by Me**

STEP BY STEP:
GETTING THE MOST OUT OF YOUR HOSPITAL STAY

- ❑ Set up a filing system.
- ❑ Create a work sheet to record hospital expenses.
- ❑ Check—and recheck—all medical bills for errors.
- ❑ Submit claims to your insurance company.
- ❑ Pay bills for uninsured expenses.
- ❑ Complain about overcharges and billing errors, if necessary.

RESOURCES:
WHERE TO GO FOR MORE INFORMATION

BOOKS

■ **Getting the Most for Your Medical Dollar**, by Charles B. Inlander and Karla Morales. Cost: $15.95, plus $2 postage and handling. Contact: Random House, Order Department, 400 Hahn Road, Westminster, MD 21157; (800) 733-3000.

■ **The Health Insurance Claims Kit**, by Carolyn Shear and Elliot Shear. Cost: $19.95, plus $4 shipping and handling. Contact: Dearborn Financial Publishing, Inc., 520 North Dearborn Street, Chicago, IL 60610-4354, (800) 252-0866.

■ **The Savvy Patient**, by David Stutz. Cost: $14.95, plus $2.50 shipping and handling. Contact: Consumer Reports Books, 9180 LeSaint Drive, Fairfield, OH 45014; (800) 272-0722.

■ **Your Complete Medical Record**, by the People's Medical Society. Cost: $12.95, plus $3 shipping and handling. Contact: People's Medical Society, 462 Walnut Street, Allentown, PA 18102; (800) 624-8773, (215) 770-1670.

■ **Your Medical Rights: How to Become an Empowered Consumer**, by Charles Inlander and Eugene I. Pavalon. Cost: $14.95, plus $3 shipping and handling. Contact: Little, Brown and Company, Attention: Order Department, 200 West Street, Waltham, MA 02154; (800) 759-0190.

ORGANIZATIONS OF INTEREST

- **National Women's Health Resource Center**, 2440 M Street NW, Suite 325, Washington, DC 20037; (202) 293-6045.

STATE DEPARTMENTS OF HEALTH

Note: Address and telephone numbers sometimes change. If you have difficulty locating the department in your state, check with the Association of State and Territorial Health Officials, 415 Second Street NE, Suite 200, Washington, DC 20002; (202) 546-5400.

ALABAMA
Department of Public Health
434 Monroe Street
Montgomery, AL 36130-3017
(205) 613-5300

ALASKA
Division of Public Health
P.O. Box H
Juneau, AK 99811-0610
(907) 465-3030

ARIZONA
Department of Health Services
1740 West Adams Street
Phoenix, AZ 85007
(602) 542-1000

ARKANSAS
Department of Health
4815 West Markham Street
Little Rock, AR 72205-9978
(501) 661-2112

CALIFORNIA
Department of Health Services
714 P Street, Room 1253
Sacramento, CA 95814
(916) 445-4171

COLORADO
Department of Health
4300 Cherry Creek Drive South
Denver, CO 80222-1530
(303) 692-2000

CONNECTICUT
Department of Health Services
150 Washington Street
Hartford, CT 06106
(203) 566-2038

DELAWARE
Division of Public Health
805 River Road
Dover, DE 19901
(302) 739-4726

DISTRICT OF COLUMBIA
Department of Public Health
1660 L Street NW, 12th Floor
Washington, DC 20036
(202) 673-7700

FLORIDA
Department of Health and
    Rehabilitative Services
1323 Winewood Boulevard, #115
Tallahassee, FL 32399-0700
(904) 488-9875

GEORGIA
Division of Public Health
2 Peachtree Street NE, Room 7-300
Atlanta, GA 30303
(404) 894-7505

HAWAII
Department of Health
Kinau Hale
P.O. Box 3378
Honolulu, HI 96801
(808) 586-4400

IDAHO
Department of Health and Welfare
450 West State Street, 10th Floor
Boise, ID 83720-5450
(208) 334-5500

ILLINOIS
Department of Public Health
535 West Jefferson Street
Springfield, IL 62761
(217) 782-4977

INDIANA
State Board of Health
1330 West Michigan Street
P.O. Box 1964
Indianapolis, IN 46202-1964
(317) 633-0100

IOWA
Department of Public Health
Lucas State Office Building
321 East 12th Street
Des Moines, IA 50319-0075
(515) 281-5787

KANSAS
Department of Health and
    Environment
900 SW Jackson, Room 620
Topeka, KS 66612
(913) 296-1500

KENTUCKY
Department of Health Services
275 East Main Street
Frankfort, KY 40621
(502) 564-3970

LOUISIANA
State Office Building
P.O. Box 0630
New Orleans, LA 70160
(504) 568-5050

MAINE
Bureau of Health
State House Station #11
Augusta, ME 04333
(207) 287-3201

MARYLAND
Department of Health and Mental
   Hygiene
201 West Preston Street
Baltimore, MD 21201
(410) 225-6860

MASSACHUSETTS
Department of Public Health
150 Tremont Street, 10th Floor
Boston, MA 02111
(617) 727-0201

MICHIGAN
Department of Public Health
3423 Martin Luther King Jr. Blvd.
P.O. Box 30195
Lansing, MI 48909
(517) 335-8000

MINNESOTA
Department of Health
717 Delaware Street SE
Minneapolis, MN 55440
(612) 623-5000

MISSISSIPPI
State Health Department
2423 North State Street
P.O. Box 1700
Jackson, MS 39215
(601) 960-7400

MISSOURI
Department of Health
P.O. Box 570
Jefferson City, MO 65102
(314) 751-6400

MONTANA
Department of Health and
   Environmental Services
P.O. Box 200901
Cogswell Building
Helena, MT 59620-0901
(406) 444-2544

NEBRASKA
Department of Health
301 Centennial Mall South
Lincoln, NE 68509
(402) 471-2133

NEVADA
Department of Health
505 East King Street
Carson City, NV 89710
(702) 687-4740

NEW HAMPSHIRE
Department of Health and
   Human Services
Health and Welfare Building
6 Hazen Drive
Concord, NH 03301-6527
(603) 271-4685

NEW JERSEY
Department of Health
CN 360
Trenton, NJ 08625
(609) 292-7837

NEW MEXICO
Department of Health
1190 St. Francis Drive
Santa Fe, NM 87503
(505) 827-2613

NEW YORK
New York State Health Department
Empire State Plaza—Corning Tower
Albany, NY 12237
(518) 474-2121

NORTH CAROLINA
Division of Health Services
Department of Environment,
   Health, and Natural Resources
P.O. Box 27687
Raleigh, NC 27611-7687
(919) 733-7081

NORTH DAKOTA
Department of Health
600 East Boulevard Avenue
Bismarck, ND 58505-0200
(701) 224-2370

OHIO
Department of Health
246 North High Street
Columbus, OH 43216-0588
(614) 466-3543

OKLAHOMA
Department of Health
1000 NE 10th Street
Oklahoma City, OK 73117
(405) 271-4200

OREGON
Health Division
800 NE Oregon, #21
Portland, OR 97232
(503) 731-4000

PENNSYLVANIA
Department of Health
P.O. Box 90,
Health & Welfare Building,
   Room 802
Harrisburg, PA 17108
(717) 787-6436

RHODE ISLAND
Department of Health
Cannon Building, Room 401
3 Capitol Hill
Providence, RI 02908-5097
(401) 277-2231

SOUTH CAROLINA
Department of Health and
   Environmental Control
2600 Bull Street
Columbia, SC 29201
(803) 734-4880

SOUTH DAKOTA
Department of Health
445 East Capitol
Pierre, SD 57501-3185
(605) 773-3361

TENNESSEE
Department of Public Health
312 8th Ave. North
Tennessee Towers
Nashville, TN 37247-0101
(615) 741-3111

TEXAS
Texas Department of Health
1100 West 49th Street
Austin, TX 78756
(512) 458-7111

UTAH
Department of Health
288 North 1460 West
Salt Lake City, UT 84116
(801) 538-6101

VERMONT
State Health Department
108 Cherry Street
Burlington, VT 05402
(802) 863-7200

VIRGINIA
State Health Department
P.O. Box 2448
Richmond, VA 23218
(804) 786-3561

WASHINGTON
Department of Health
1300 SE Quince Street
P.O. Box 47890
Olympia, WA 98504-7890
(206) 586-5846

WEST VIRGINIA
Department of Health
Building 3, Room 519
State Capitol Complex
Charleston, WV 25305-0501
(304) 558-2971

WISCONSIN
Division of Health Services
121 East Wilson Street
P.O. Box 7894
Madison, WI 53707-7984
(608) 266-7568

WYOMING
Department of Health and
    Human Services
117 Hathaway Building
Cheyenne, WY 82002
(307) 777-7656

STATE MEDICAL LICENSING BOARDS

ALABAMA
Alabama Medical Licensure
    Commission
P.O. Box 887
Montgomery, AL 36101-0887
(205) 242-4153

ALASKA
Alaska Department of Commerce
    and Economic Development
Division of Occupational Licensing
State Medical Board
P.O. Box 110806
Juneau, AK 99811
(907) 465-2541

ARIZONA
Arizona Board of Medical Examiners
1651 E. Morten Avenue, Suite 210
Phoenix, AZ 85020
(602) 255-3751

ARKANSAS
Arkansas Board of
    Medical Examiners
2100 Riverfront Drive, Suite 200
Little Rock, AR 72202
(501) 324-9410

CALIFORNIA
California Board of Medical Quality
    Assurance
1426 Howe Avenue
Sacramento, CA 95825
(916) 263-2388

COLORADO
Colorado Board of Medical
    Examiners
1560 Broadway, Suite 1300
Denver, CO 80202
(303) 894-7690

CONNECTICUT
Connecticut Board of Medical
    Examiners
150 Washington Street
Hartford, CT 06106
(203) 566-1035

DELAWARE
Delaware Board of Medical Practice
O'Neil Building
P.O. Box 1401, Suite 203
Dover, DE 19903
(302) 739-4522

DISTRICT OF COLUMBIA
District of Columbia Occupational
    and Professional Licensing
    Administration
605 G Street NW
Lower Level 202
Washington, DC 20001
(202) 727-7480

FLORIDA
Florida Board of Medical Examiners
1940 N. Monroe Street
Tallahassee, FL 32399-0770
(904) 488-0595

GEORGIA
Georgia Composite State Board of
    Medical Examiners
166 Pryor Street SW, Room 424
Atlanta, GA 30303
(404) 656-3913

HAWAII
Hawaii Board of Medical Examiners
Department of Commerce and
    Consumer Affairs
P.O. Box 3469
Honolulu, HI 96801
(808) 586-2708

IDAHO
Idaho State Board of Medicine
280 North 8th Street, Suite 202
State House Mail
Boise, ID 83720
(208) 334-2822

ILLINOIS
Illinois Department of Professional
    Registration
320 W. Washington Street
Springfield, IL 62786
(217) 785-0800

INDIANA
Indiana Attorney General/
    Consumer Protection Division
402 W. Washington Street
Indianapolis, IN 46204
(317) 232-6330

IOWA
Iowa State Board of
  Medical Examiners
1209 East Court Avenue
Executive Hills West
Des Moines, IA 50319
(515) 281-5171

KANSAS
Kansas State Board of Healing Arts
235 SW Topeka Boulevard
Topeka, KS 66603-3058
(913) 296-7413

KENTUCKY
Kentucky Board of Medical
  Licensure
310 Whittington Parkway, Suite 1-B
Louisville, KY 40222
(502) 429-8046

LOUISIANA
Louisiana State Board of
  Medical Examiners
830 Union Street, Suite 100
New Orleans, LA 70112
(504) 524-6763

MAINE
Maine Board of Registration in
  Medicine
State House Station #137
Augusta, ME 04333
(207) 287-3601

MARYLAND
Maryland Physician Quality
  Assurance
P.O. Box 2571
Baltimore, MD 21215-0095
(410) 764-4777

MASSACHUSETTS
Massachusetts Board of Registration
  in Medicine
10 West Street
Boston, MA 02111
(617) 727-3086

MICHIGAN
Michigan Board of Medicine
Bureau of Occupational and
  Professional Regulation
Department of Commerce
Attention: Medical Board
P.O. Box 30018
Lansing, MI 48909-7518
(517) 373-1870

MINNESOTA
Minnesota State Board of Medical
  Practice
2700 University Avenue West,
  Suite 106
St. Paul, MN 55114-1080
(612) 642-0538

MISSISSIPPI
Mississippi State Board of Medical
  Licensure
2688-D Insurance Center Drive
Jackson, MI 39216
(601) 354-6645

MISSOURI
Missouri State Board of Registration
  for the Healing Arts
P.O. Box 4
Jefferson City, MO 65102
(314) 751-0098

MONTANA
Montana Board of
    Medical Examiners
111 North Jackson
P.O. Box 200513
Helena, MT 59620-0513
(406) 444-4284

NEBRASKA
Nebraska Board of
    Medical Examiners
301 Centennial Mall South
P.O. Box 95007
Lincoln, NE 68509-5007
(402) 471-2115

NEVADA
Nevada State Board of
    Medical Examiners
P.O. Box 7238
Reno, NV 89510
(702) 688-2559

NEW HAMPSHIRE
New Hampshire Board of
    Registration in Medicine
Health and Welfare Building
6 Hazen Drive
Concord, NH 03301
(603) 271-1203

NEW JERSEY
New Jersey State Board of
    Medical Examiners
140 East Front Street
Trenton, NJ 08608
(609) 292-4843

NEW MEXICO
New Mexico Board of
    Medical Examiners
491 Old Santa Fe Trail
Lamy Building, 2nd Floor
Santa Fe, NM 87501
(505) 827-9933

NEW YORK
New York State Department
    of Health
Office of Professional
    Medical Conduct
Empire State Plaza
Corning Tower Building, Room 438
Albany, NY 12237
(518) 474-8357

NORTH CAROLINA
North Carolina Board of
    Medical Examiners
P.O. Box 20007
Raleigh, NC 27619
(919) 828-1212

NORTH DAKOTA
North Dakota State Board of
    Medical Examiners
418 East Broadway, Suite 12
Bismarck, ND 58501
(701) 223-9485

OHIO
Ohio State Medical Board
77 South High Street, 17th Floor
Columbus, OH 43266-0315
(614) 466-3938

OKLAHOMA
Oklahoma State Board of
   Medical Examiners
5104 North Francis Street, Suite C
Oklahoma City, OK 73118
(405) 848-6841

OREGON
Oregon State Board of
   Medical Examiners
1500 SW First Avenue, Suite 620
Portland, OR 97201-5826
   (503) 229-5770

PENNSYLVANIA
Pennsylvania State Board of Medical
   Education and Licensure
P.O. Box 2649
Harrisburg, PA 17105-2649
(717) 787-2381

RHODE ISLAND
Rhode Island Division of
   Professional Regulation
Rhode Island Department of Health
3 Capitol Hill, Room 104
Providence, RI 02908
(401) 277-2827

SOUTH CAROLINA
South Carolina State Board of
   Medical Examiners
P.O. Box 212269
Columbia, SC 29211
(803) 731-1650

SOUTH DAKOTA
South Dakota State Board of Medical
   and Osteopathic Examiners
1323 South Minnesota Avenue
Sioux Falls, SD 57105
(605) 336-1965

TENNESSEE
Tennessee Board of
   Medical Examiners
283 Plus Park Boulevard
Nashville, TN 37247-1010
   (615) 367-6231

TEXAS
Texas Board of Medical Examiners
P.O. Box 149134
Austin, TX 78714-9134
(512) 834-7728

UTAH
Utah Department of Commerce
Division of Occupational and
   Professional Licensing
160 East 300 South
P.O. Box 45805
Salt Lake City, UT 84145
(801) 530-6628

VERMONT
Vermont Board of Medical Practice
109 State Street
Montpelier, VT 05609-1106
(802) 828-2673

VIRGINIA
Virginia State Board of Medicine
6606 West Broad Street, 4th Floor
Richmond, VA 23230-1717
(804) 662-9908

WASHINGTON
Washington State Medical Boards
Board of Medical Examiners
1300 Quince
Olympia, WA 98504-7866
(206) 753-2205

WEST VIRGINIA
West Virginia Board of Medicine
101 Dee Drive
Charleston, WV 25311
(304) 558-2921

WISCONSIN
Wisconsin Medical Examining Board
P.O. Box 8935
Madison, WI 53708
(608) 266-2811

WYOMING
Wyoming Board of Medicine
Barrett Building, Room 208
2301 Central Avenue
Cheyenne, WY 82002
(307) 777-6463

GLOSSARY: UNDERSTANDING THE TERMS

Assignment: An agreement by a doctor or health-care facility to accept the "reasonable and customary" charges established by the insurance company as the total payment for service.

Coinsurance or co-payment: The portion of your medical bill that you share with the insurance company after you have paid the deductible. For example, if your policy calls for a $100 deductible and 20 percent co-insurance, you pay the first $100 and 20 percent of all subsequent medical bills up to the limit established in your policy.

Deductible: The amount of money you must pay before your insurance coverage kicks in. A policy with a $100 deductible means that you pay $100 each year before the insurance company pays a cent.

Reasonable and customary: The fee established by the insurance company as fair compensation for a medical service. For example, the insurance company might consider $250 the reasonable and customary charge for a sonogram, meaning any charges in excess of that amount would have to be paid by the patient.

Stop-loss: A cap on the amount you will have to pay. With a $2,000 stop-loss provision, you will have to pay the deductible and the co-payment up to the $2,000 limit. Once you have paid $2,000 in medical expenses for the year, the insurance company picks up the tab to 100 percent of the rest. Also called an out-of-pocket limit.

CHAPTER 7

SOMEONE TO WATCH OVER YOU

Choosing the Best Child Care for Your Family

NUTS AND BOLTS

It's tough to leave your child in someone else's care. But in many cases both parents must—or choose to—return to the workplace, making some form of child care a necessity. The question then becomes: Taking cost into consideration, which child-care option is best for the family?

The universe of child care breaks down into two categories: away-from-home care and at-home care. *Away-from-home care* can be provided by day-care centers or family day care. *At-home care* includes nannies, au pairs, and old-fashioned baby-sitters. Each alternative has advantages and disadvantages—including a wide range of costs. In many households child care is one of the biggest-ticket items in the family budget.

In general, away-from-home care is cheaper than at-home care because your child shares a caretaker with a number of other children. This group setting provides your child with a chance to play with other kids, as well as a chance to enjoy different activities and games than those available at home. Parents enjoy the stability of care—no last-minute calls from a baby-sitter who is sick or stuck in a snowstorm. On the other hand, the chance to play with other kids means the chance to share germs and illnesses with other kids. And while a day-care center might not close its doors because a caretaker gets sick, it will shut down during certain holidays and vacation periods, even if you have to make it to work that day. The cost of away-from-home care depends on whether you choose a day-care center, which can cost $200 a week, or family day care, which costs about $150 a week. (Prices vary widely but tend to be higher in metropolitan areas.)

At-home care allows for one-on-one attention between your child and a caretaker. Because the caretaker is working just for you, she or he will probably be able to work around your schedule, including an occasional breakfast meeting or evening reception. And for this custom service you pay a premium. Trained nannies can cost $250 a week, plus room and board; European au pairs cost $100 a week, plus transportation and other fees, which bring the total cost to around $170 a week. If you are the parent of an infant, you may prefer at-home care because there is a greater chance for a strong, healthy relationship to develop between your child and the caregiver. Continuity of care can be important in providing your child with a secure and stable environment. It may also create the risk that your child will suffer a significant loss if a beloved mother substitute quits or if you must let her go.

Whatever type of child care you're considering, start by collecting references from other parents, your pediatrician, members of your church or synagogue, local hospitals, and senior citizen organizations, in addition to checking out the listings under "day care" and "baby-sitting services" in your local phone book. Also use the organizations listed in the Resources section of this chapter to track down nannies, au pairs, and licensed day-care centers and family day-care homes.

If Mom is planning to return to work after a short maternity leave, she should begin to plan for day care before the baby is born. Finding the ideal caretaker or child-care arrangement can be a time-consuming process, so allow at least two months for the search. And keep in mind that some places won't take a reservation—you may have to wait until you're ready for placement to enroll your child.

AWAY FROM HOME

When it comes to away-from-home child care, you have two main options: home or family day care and group care at a day-care center. It's hard to compare a simple home-care situation—a mother taking two or three children into her home—with the setup in a day-care center that has 10 instructors, a playground cluttered with gym equipment, and a fully stocked arts and crafts center, but both are types of away-from-home child care.

HOME OR FAMILY DAY CARE

Many parents feel more comfortable leaving their children, especially babies, in a family situation in a private home.

Advantages
- Provides a warm, homelike environment;
- Usually cheaper than at-home care or many day-care centers;
- Less exposure to germs and infection than in group day-care centers;
- More potential for individual attention and stimulation because there are fewer children;
- Flexible scheduling and hours may be available.

Disadvantages
- The facility may be unlicensed; most states only require licensing for facilities that accommodate six or more children. If a facility is unlicensed, you have no guarantee that it follows prescribed health and safety regulations;
- Care providers are often untrained and may not have practice dealing with a number of children;
- Care provider's child-care philosophy may differ from yours;
- No backup when your child is sick;
- No backup when the care provider or one of her children is sick.

Questions to Ask a Prospective Family Day-Care Provider
- Why did you decide to open a family day-care home?
- Are you licensed?
- Why have you decided to accept another child at this time?
- What is the total number of children in your care? Is this a maximum?
- What is the age range of children in your care?
- What do you find most difficult about raising children?
- How do you discipline the children? What kinds of rewards and punishments do you use?
- What is the daily routine for children in your care?
- Where do the children play? Nap? Snack?
- Do the children watch television? If so, which programs?
- What do you fix for lunch and snacks?
- What other members of your family will be in the household?
- Will they be in contact with the children?
- Do you provide backup care when you are sick?
- When do you usually take your vacation and for how long?
- Do I need to bring any toys or other equipment for my child?
- What is the payment schedule?
- Do you have any pets?
- Do you smoke? Drink alcohol?
- Do you accept frozen breast milk?
- May I have names of other parents as references?
- Do you have training in infant CPR? First aid?
- How would you handle tears? Tantrums? Fights?
- What is the agenda for a typical day?
- Is parental visitation allowed without prior notice?
- How often are diapers changed?
- Do the children go outside every day?

GROUP DAY CARE

A good day-care center can provide a stimulating environment and good social interaction for your children.

Advantages
- Trained personnel may provide an organized program customized to your baby's development and growth;

- Your child can play with other babies and children;
- Backup care is available if a teacher becomes sick or leaves;
- Licensed day-care centers must meet certain safety and health standards, and in some states educational standards as well. (Keep in mind that licensing is no guarantee of quality care.)

Disadvantages
- There may be fixed hours of operation: less flexibility in scheduling;
- If the center follows a public school calendar, it may be closed on some days when you need to work;
- Your child will be exposed to the germs of the other children in the center;
- The costs are usually fairly high (less than in-home care and more than family day care).

Questions to Ask a Prospective Day-Care Center Administrator
- Is the center licensed by the state?
- What kind of insurance do you have?
- What is the payment schedule?
- Do you offer discounts for more than one child?
- Do I get credit when my child is sick or on vacation?
- Is your day-care center affiliated with any religious group or other organization?
- What is your center's philosophy about child care?
- Will a crying infant be tended to immediately?
- What is your center's philosophy about discipline?
- How do you handle tears? Tantrums? Fights?
- Does the center have a formal educational program?
- How many full-time children attend the center? Part-time?
- What is the adult-to-child ratio for infants? Toddlers? Preschoolers?
- Do the children go outside every day?
- What are the daily routines?
- How often are diapers changed?
- Are the babies kept in their cribs all day?
- Are the children separated by age group?
- Do the children have a rest period every day?

- What training and education is required of the staff?
- How many teachers have been on the staff for more than one year?
- How do you monitor the staff?
- Are members of the staff required to wash their hands after every diaper change?
- How often are the children's toys washed with a sanitizing solution?
- Are all the children immunized?
- What is your policy toward sick children coming to the center?
- How many outbreaks of illness (more serious than a cold) have occurred in the past year?
- What is the center's policy regarding administering medicines during the day?
- Are there any doctors or nurses on staff?
- What are the notification procedures if my child is injured?
- Are parents expected to provide lunches and changes of clothing?
- What kind of snacks will be served during the day?
- Does the center have an active parent board that is involved in the operation of the program?
- Do you have parent-teacher conferences?
- Do you give written progress reports?
- Do parents volunteer as classroom helpers or aides?
- May I have the names of other parents as references?
- Is parental visitation allowed without prior notice?

AT HOME

Many parents feel that if a parent can't be with the child all the time, then the next-best option is a parent substitute—either a nanny, an au pair, or a baby-sitter/housekeeper. Keep in mind that in addition to the obvious costs of salary or stipend, live-in home care has hidden costs: increased food and insurance costs, taxes, and perhaps renovation costs for work done to provide living space for the care provider.

Nannies are child-care specialists, hired specifically to care for children. They can live in or out—and they may or may not arrive via flying umbrella and sing like Julie Andrews. Many nannies, especially the expensive ones, have professional training in child development, health and nutrition, and first aid. Nannies are top-of-the-line child care, as the price tag shows. They often cost about $250 a week, plus room and board; wages are higher for those who live out.

There are about a dozen nanny schools nationwide (and more overseas); in the United States the American Council of Nanny Schools accredits nanny programs. For a list of accredited schools and their placement services see the listing for the American Council of Nanny Schools in the Resources section of this chapter.

Au pair is a French word meaning "on par" or "as an equal." The idea is to exchange services—40 to 45 hours a week of child care for room and board and a modest stipend, about $100 a week or so. Foreign au pairs are usually untrained 18- to 25-year-olds who are eager to spend time abroad. By definition the jobs are temporary—no more than one year—which can present a problem for young children who might develop an attachment to an au pair and suffer an emotional loss when he or she leaves. There are also some American au pairs who do the same work, but because they don't need visas or permission to work, they can stay with a family for more than one year. Only a handful of au pair placement agencies are authorized to bring foreign au pairs into the United States to work. (See the Resources section for a list of qualified agencies as well as information on how to contact the U.S. Information Agency's Office of Exchange Visitor Program Services.)

Baby-sitters provide child care, along with some light housekeeping in many cases. Finding the right baby-sitter is largely a matter of luck: some love children and provide responsible, attentive care; others don't. The best way to find the right sitter is to leave yourself enough time to search until you find the right match.

When defining the role of your sitter/housekeeper, go easy on assigning household chores. You have undoubtedly found it difficult to watch your children and clean the house at the same time, and the job doesn't get any easier just because you're paying someone else to do it. When someone who is working for you has too much to do, often the cleaning gets done at the child's expense because you're more apt to notice the dishes in the sink than the smile on your child's face after an exciting day spent walking in the woods.

Advantages
- Your child is kept in familiar surroundings;
- Minimal disruption of your child's daily schedule;
- No exposure to other babies' germs;
- Care is available even when your child is sick;
- No hassles transporting your child back and forth to day care;
- Your child gets plenty of individual attention from the caregiver (assuming you've kept housekeeping tasks to a minimum);
- Parents set the hours;
- The relationship is long term and stable;
- You have more control over the type of care your child receives: the use of discipline, punishments, rewards, etc.;
- If you have an older child in school, the caregiver can take care of him or her after school.

Disadvantages
- No backup care if the caregiver is sick, unable to come to work for other reasons, or suddenly quits;
- Your child can become very attached to the caretaker, resulting in an emotional loss if the sitter leaves suddenly;
- Parents may become jealous if the child and the caregiver develop a close relationship;
- Parents must forgo some privacy if the caregiver lives in the home;
- Your child may be isolated from other children;
- It's up to parents to recognize quality care since there is no licensing of at-home care;
- The caregiver is unsupervised;
- In-home care tends to be more expensive than other alternatives;
- Parents must pay taxes and file paperwork for employees (see page 145).

Questions to Ask a Prospective At-Home Caregiver
- Why do you want this job?
- What experience have you had taking care of children?
- What was your last job like?
- Why did you leave?
- How long do you expect to stay with this job?

- Do you have children of your own? How will their needs interfere with your work?
- Have you had (are you willing to take) infant CPR? First aid?
- Do you drive? If not, how would you get to work? What would you do in an emergency?
- Do you smoke? Drink alcohol?
- Would you be able to come early or stay late on occasion?
- Which religious holidays or other days would you need off?
- What kind of things do you like doing with children?
- How do you see yourself spending the day with my baby?
- How do you see your role in my baby's life?
- How do you believe children should be disciplined?
- How would you handle tears? Tantrums? Fights?
- How do you feel about physical affection?
- What do you think a child the age of mine needs most?
- Do you do housework?
- Would you take care of the family pet?

HELP ON HIRING HELP

Finding the right child-care provider is a lot of work. The following tips may help you find the right person for your situation the first time you hire:

■ **Define the job**. Before you begin the search for the perfect Mary Poppins, make sure you know exactly what you want the person to do. Do you want the person to do shopping and laundry? Cooking and cleaning? You need to let the prospective employee know exactly what is expected by explicitly defining the responsibilities of the job.

■ **Get the word out**. Ask everyone you know for recommendations and referrals. Talk to your pediatrician, to parents, to teachers in preschools. Place an advertisement in local newspapers, college employment offices, church or synagogue bulletins, and senior citizen centers. Look at the listings under "child care" and "baby-sitting" in your local phone book. Get information from au pair and nanny organizations (see pages 153–154).

In your advertisement be sure to include the number of children and their ages, the hours you need help, and the salary. List a phone number with an answering machine so that you can screen calls as they come in.

■ **Screen by phone**. You'd be surprised at what you can learn about people by talking to them on the phone. Ask a lot of "what if" questions: What would you do if my child started screaming because she didn't want me to go to work? What would you do if my child wanted an extra cookie at lunchtime? What would you do if my baby cried for half an hour for no apparent reason? If you have any reservations about a prospective caretaker after the phone interview, don't bother asking her to your home for a personal interview. You need to trust her judgment completely.

■ **Interview in person**. Ask the prospective employee to come to your home for a face-to-face interview. Ask many of the same questions you did on the phone, keeping your eyes open to subtle clues that might indicate more about her. How did she respond when she met the child or children? Does she seem to like kids? Listen to the questions she asks you: if she asks whether the child cries a lot, she may be telling you that she won't be very patient with a fussy baby (as all babies are from time to time). Did she show up on time? Was she clean and well groomed? Did you like her? Did you trust her? At a certain point you must trust your gut instincts: if the person just "feels wrong" for the job, she probably is.

■ **Check out all the references**. Ask your final candidates for a list of references. If you're not sure whether a reference is valid or not, ask some open-ended questions that you have already asked the prospective caretaker. For example, ask, How long did she work for you? How much did you pay her? How many children do you have? What are their ages? If the reference is bogus, you'll usually be able to tell because the person will probably be unprepared to answer all your questions accurately.

■ **Allow for a period of adjustment**. If possible, have the caretaker spend at least a day watching and helping you with the baby. Explain how you want things done, where you keep the necessary supplies, and what your attitudes are about child care and child rearing. If you have the luxury of time, ease your sitter—and the baby—into the new routine by spending an hour away, then two hours, gradually lengthening the time the two spend together on their own.

■ **Keep the arrangement on a trial basis until you're sure it will work**. Tell your caretaker that you would like the first two weeks or month to be a probationary period, just to make sure the arrangement works to everyone's satisfaction. Let your baby decide whether or not the arrangement works: Is he or she happy at the end of the day? Does he or she seem more tired and cranky than usual? Or more alert and attentive? Does your baby have diaper rash? Does he or she seem clean? Again, your instincts can probably tell you within the trial period whether you've found a workable arrangement or not.

OTHER OPTIONS

If you don't need regular child care, just a sitter now and then, you may not need to go through the hassle of arranging for formal child care. In this case you might consider such solutions as

- Hiring a part-time college student;
- Asking a neighbor or a parent from your childbirth education class to baby-sit either for money or in exchange for taking care of her child at a designated time;
- Dropping your child at a church group "parents' day out" program, which allows you to get a little time to yourself while your child gets a chance to play with other kids his or her age;
- Starting a baby-sitting co-op: in a co-op a group of parents get together and take turns baby-sitting for one another;
- Asking Grandma or another relative to baby-sit on a regular basis. If you want to make a regular date, try to make the arrangement more formal by paying for the service.

KEEPING IT LEGAL

If you choose to have an at-home caregiver, you will become an employer and you will be legally required to pay taxes and file several

THE BABY-SITTER CHECKLIST

Even the best baby-sitter needs instructions. Before you leave your baby with anyone, make certain that the sitter is familiar with the following:

Tonight's Plan

- ❑ Where you are going;
- ❑ The phone number where you will be;
- ❑ When you plan to return home.

Phone List

- ❑ Your name, address, and phone number (with a written statement of directions of how to get there);
- ❑ Name, address, and phone number of a relative or friend;
- ❑ Name, address, and phone number of a neighbor;
- ❑ Name, address, and phone number of your pediatrician;
- ❑ Fire department;
- ❑ Police emergency;
- ❑ Poison control center;
- ❑ Ambulance service;
- ❑ Nearest hospital emergency room (with directions of how to get there);
- ❑ Taxi company (location of cab fare in case of emergency).

Information List

- ❑ To calm the baby . . .
- ❑ My baby's favorite toy is . . .
- ❑ My baby likes to sleep . . .
- ❑ My baby is best burped . . .
- ❑ To diaper and clean the baby . . .
- ❑ Extra clothing is kept . . .
- ❑ To give my baby a bottle or food . . .
- ❑ My baby should not eat . . .
- ❑ My child can watch television only . . .
- ❑ At bedtime my child enjoys . . .
- ❑ If my child wakes up in the night . . .
- ❑ No one is allowed to visit except . . .

forms with various government agencies. Because of the paperwork burden and increased cost, an estimated three-quarters of all Americans who hire in-home child care and domestic workers ignore the rules. Being a good citizen and paying the taxes can add as much as 10 to 20 percent to the base wages you pay, but it will help you clear an important hurdle if you ever want to be appointed attorney general or run for public office. It is also the law.

If you hire a foreign au pair, you don't need to file any of this paperwork: you're paying the agency to handle the hassles. However, if you independently hire an American au pair, it's just like hiring any other kind of household help, and the rules do apply. To keep it all on the up-and-up, be aware of the following:

Income Taxes

You don't have to withhold income tax on wages paid to a household employee unless you and your employee agree to do it. For the most up-to-date information on reporting requirements for income, call the Internal Revenue Service at (800) 829-3676. Start out by asking for IRS Publication 503, "Child and Dependent Care Expenses," and Publication 926, "Employment Taxes for Household Employers." These two booklets will tell you just about everything you need to know. Any questions you have can be answered by the IRS tax hotline at (800) 829-1040.

Basically every quarter you will have to fill out Form 942 for Social Security tax, income tax, and Medicare. Once a year you'll have to fill out two forms—Form 940 (or 940-EZ) for unemployment tax and a W-2 form reporting the employee's earnings for the year. You'll give a copy of the W-2 to your employee and another to the Social Security office (which then shares the information with the IRS). If you hire more than one employee, you'll have to fill out a W-3 form, which is very much like the W-2.

The only other form you may have to file with the IRS is Form SS-4. You'll need an employer identification number to report the taxes and to issue the tax statements, and you use Form SS-4 to obtain the number, but you'll only have to do that once. You should not use your personal Social Security number in place of the employer identification number.

Social Security and Medicare Taxes

If you pay someone more than $50 within a three-month period, you must pay Social Security and Medicare taxes on those wages under the Federal Insurance Contribution Act (FICA). The payments (or contributions) must be made every calendar quarter. Both you and your employee are expected to pay equally to the Social Security tax. You could leave it up to your child-care provider to pay her share, but be aware that if she fails to pay, the government will later hold you responsible for her share—and charge you a penalty, too. To avoid this possibility, most parents who pay Social Security either pay the entire amount for their caregivers (which increases the amount on which the tax is calculated) or withhold the employee's share by deducting it from her pay.

You don't have to fill out any additional paperwork to pay the Social Security tax: it's part of the IRS form 942 that you'll already be filling out to report the income tax. For 1993 the Social Security tax rate is 12.4 percent (6.2 percent from you, 6.2 percent from your care provider); the Medicare rate is 2.9 percent (1.45 percent from you, 1.45 percent from your care provider).

Unemployment Tax

If you pay someone more than $1,000 within a three-month period, you must pay Federal Unemployment Tax (FUTA). Payments are reported annually to the IRS using Form 940 or 940-EZ. Call the IRS for the proper forms. The rate is 6.2 percent through 1996. It is paid by the employer, not the employee.

Some states require employers to pay a state unemployment tax as well. Call your state unemployment commission for more information. In most cases if you must pay the state, you can take a credit against your federal unemployment tax.

Worker's Compensation

Worker's compensation is a form of insurance coverage that many states require for household employers whether or not the worker lives in the home. It covers your liabilities if your child-care provider is injured while working in your home. The annual cost varies from state to state, but it typically runs from $200 to $400.

You should also contact your personal insurance agent to find out if you are covered by the liability provision of your existing homeowner's or renter's insurance policy. In some states you are required to have a separate policy if you employ someone in your home. Your insurance agent should be able to provide more information on your coverage.

Immigration Papers

In 1986 Congress passed the Immigration Reform and Control Act, which says that you can legally hire only American citizens or aliens who are authorized to work in the United States. As an employer it's up to you to verify that any individual you hire is either an American citizen or eligible to work here legally.

It's not enough simply to ask your caregiver if she is a citizen or ask to see her "green card" (which, by the way, is no longer green). Instead you must complete U.S. Immigration and Naturalization Service Form I-9, Employment Eligibility Verification, for *anyone* you hire, regardless of his or her nationality. Both you and the caregiver must sign the form. You must also see actual proof of eligibility for employment, including a Social Security card, a U.S. passport, an alien registration card, or some other picture ID, such as a driver's license or student ID card.

For more information contact the U.S. Department of Justice, Immigration and Naturalization Service, at (800) 755-0777; ask for the Employer's Handbook and a copy of Form I-9.

Car Insurance Premiums

Check with your auto insurance agent to find out whether your caregiver should be added to your auto insurance policy.

Other Taxes

You also may have to pay local or state taxes. Check with an accountant or local tax department for the requirements, if any, in your area.

ISSUES TO DISCUSS:
WHAT PARENTS SHOULD TALK ABOUT

- ❑ How much can we afford to spend on child care?
- ❑ How many days a week do we need help? How many hours a day?
- ❑ Do we want at-home child care?
- ❑ Live-in care? A long-term nanny? A one-year au pair?
- ❑ Away-from-home care? A day-care center? Family day care?
- ❑ Who will be responsible for interviewing prospective caretakers?
- ❑ Who will be responsible for visiting day-care centers and day-care homes?
- ❑ If we hire someone for home care, who will be responsible for handling the necessary paperwork?

QUESTIONS & ANSWERS

I work at a job that takes me away from the telephone for extended periods of time. How can I be sure my child will receive medical care in an emergency?

Provide your caregiver or day-care center with a signed medical release form. This form should authorize your caregiver to seek medical treatment for your child if there is an emergency and you cannot be reached. The form should contain a simple statement, such as:

I, (your name), give (caregiver's name) the authority to make emergency medical decisions regarding the care of my child, (child's name). My child is allergic to the following: _____. My medical insurance carrier is _____; the policy number is _____.

Signed:_____

Even though you may hesitate to give such broad authority to your child's caregiver, doctors and hospitals are sometimes legally unable to provide care without authorized consent. It is essential that your child have access to emergency treatment whether or not you can be reached.

I know that I am supposed to identify my child's caregiver on my tax return, but how am I supposed to do this?

On your tax return you simply list the child-care provider's name, address, and taxpayer identification number (Social Security number). You can obtain the information by having the employee fill out Internal Revenue Service Form W-10, Dependent Care Provider's Identification and Certification, or ask to see one of the following:

- A copy of the care provider's Social Security card;
- A copy of the care provider's driver's license (in a state where the license includes the Social Security number);
- A copy of the care provider's W-4 form;
- A letter or invoice from the care provider that shows the required information.

Keep this information with your records so you'll have it on hand if the IRS asks to see it. As long as you use "due diligence" in collecting the information, you won't be penalized if the care provider gives you false or incomplete information.

Do minimum-wage and other employment standards apply to child-care workers?

It depends if you have a casual or a professional child-care provider. "Casual" baby-sitters—those who work on an irregular or intermittent basis and who don't baby-sit as a vocation—don't have to receive minimum wage or overtime. Full-time baby-sitters or child-care workers enjoy the protection provided by the Fair Labor Standards Act, including the right to minimum wage and overtime pay. To obtain a free copy of the booklet "How the Fair Labor Standards Act Applies to Domestic Service Workers" write to the U.S. Department of Labor, Employment Standards Administration, Wages and Hours Division, 200 Constitution Avenue NW, Washington, DC 20210; (202) 219-4907.

Do I have to pay Social Security for my foreign au pair?

If you hire a foreign au pair, you don't have to file any paperwork with the Social Security Administration; it's up to the placement agency to handle these headaches for you. The person you hire does have to pay Social Security taxes, but this is one administrative task you don't need to worry about. If you hire an American au pair directly, then you need to pay Social Security and other taxes just as you would for any other household employee.

I have four children. Do I have to pay extra to find an au pair willing to take on the additional work?

The fees for foreign au pair programs are fixed. You pay the same rate whether you have one, two, four, or 10 children. If you hire an American au pair, it will be up to you and the caretaker to work out an equitable arrangement.

STEP BY STEP: ARRANGING FOR CHILD CARE

- ❑ Decide on what type of child care you need.
- ❑ If at-home care:
  - Advertise the position;
  - Interview candidates by phone and in person;
  - Check all references;
  - Select a child-care provider.

- ❑ If away-from-home care:
  - Get recommendations;
  - Visit facilities;
  - Interview facility administrators or family day-care providers;
  - Check references;
  - Select a facility.

- ❑ If necessary, file paperwork:
  - IRS Form 940 (or 940-EZ);
  - IRS Form 942;
  - W-2 (or W-3);
  - Immigration and Naturalization Service Form I-9.

- ❑ Check with your personal insurance agent regarding worker's compensation, liability insurance, auto insurance, etc.

RESOURCES:
WHERE TO GO FOR MORE INFORMATION

BOOKS

■ **The Complete Guide to Choosing Child Care**, by the National Association of Child Care Resource and Referral Agencies, Child Care, Inc., and Judith Berezin. Cost: $12.95, plus $2 shipping and handling. Contact: Random House, Order Department, 400 Hahn Road, Westminster, MD 21157; (800) 733-3000.

■ **Shopping for Quality Day Care**, by Claudia Bischoff. Cost: $12.95, plus $3.95 shipping and handling. Contact: Round Lake Publishing, 31 Bailey Ave., Ridgefield, CT 06877; (203) 431-9696.

BROCHURES

■ For a free copy of the brochure "Finding Good Child Care: A Checklist," contact: The Child Care Action Campaign, 330 7th Avenue, 17th Floor, New York, NY 10001; (212) 239-0138.

ORGANIZATIONS

- **American Council of Nanny Schools**, Delta College, University Center, MI 48710; (517) 686-9417.

- **Child Care Aware**, 2116 Campus Drive SE, Rochester, MN 55904; (800) 424-2246, (507) 287-2220.

- **National Association of Child Care Resource and Referral Agencies**, 1319 F Street NW, Suite 606, Washington, DC 20004; (202) 393-5501.

- **National Association for Family Day Care**, 1331-A Pennsylvania Avenue NW, Suite 348, Washington, DC 20004; (800) 359-3817.

NATIONAL AU PAIR PLACEMENT AGENCIES

For a complete list of authorized foreign au pair programs contact the U.S. Information Agency's Office of Exchange Visitor Program Services at (202) 475-2389.

- **Au Pair in America**, 102 Greenwich Ave., Greenwich, CT 06830; (800) 727-2437.

- **AuPair/Homestay USA**, 1015 15 Street NW, Suite 750, Washington, DC 20005; (202) 408-5380.

- **EF AuPair**, 1 Memorial Drive, Cambridge, MA 02142; (800) 333-6056.

- **Au Pair Programme USA**, 2469 East Fort Union Blvd., Suite 114, Salt Lake City, UT 84121; (801) 943-7788.

- **American Heritage Association**, Au Pair Intercultural, Flavia Hall, Marylhurst College Campus, P.O. Box 147, Marylhurst, OR 97036; (503) 635-3702.

- **AuPairCare**, One Post Street, 7th Floor, San Francisco, CA 94104; (800) 288-7786, (415) 434-8788.

- **EurAuPair**, 250 North Pacific Coast Highway, Laguna Beach, CA 92651; (800) 333-3804.

- **InterExchange**, 161 6th Avenue, Room 902, New York, NY 10013; (212) 924-0446.

EARLY CHILDHOOD LICENSING AUTHORITIES

ALABAMA
Office of Day Care and Child
  Development
Department of Human Resources
50 Ripley Street
Montgomery, AL 36130
(205) 242-1425

ALASKA
Child Care Unit
Division of Family and Youth
  Services
Department of Health and Social
  Services
P.O. Box 110630
Juneau, AK 99811-0630
(907) 465-2145

ARIZONA
Office of Child Day Care Facilities
Department of Health Services
1647 E. Morten Avenue, Suite 230
Phoenix, AZ 85020
(602) 255-1272

ARKANSAS
Day Care Unit
Division of Children and Family
    Services
Department of Human Services
626 Donaghey Plaza
Main and Seventh Streets
P.O. Box 1437, Slot 604
Little Rock, AR 72203-1437
(501) 682-8768

CALIFORNIA
Children's Day Care
Administrative Support Bureau
Department of Social Services
744 P Street, Mail Stop 19-50
Sacramento, CA 95814
(916) 324-4031

COLORADO
Office of Child Care Services
Colorado Department of Social
    Services
1575 Sherman Street, 1st Floor
Denver, CO 80203
(303) 866-5942

CONNECTICUT
Center and Group Home Care:
Day Care Licensing
Department of Health Services
150 Washington Street
Hartford, CT 06106
(203) 566-2575

Family Day Care Licensing
Department of Social Services
Day Care Unit
330 Broad Street
Manchester, CT 06040
(203) 646-8239

DELAWARE
Division of Child Protection
Licensing Services
Department of Services for Children,
    Youth and Their Families
1825 Faulkland Road
Wilmington, DE 19805
(302) 633-2510

DISTRICT OF COLUMBIA
Day Care Licensing
Department of Consumers and
    Regulatory Affairs
614 H Street NW, Room 1035
Washington, DC 20001
(202) 727-7226

FLORIDA
Child Care and Prevention Unit
Department of Health and
    Rehabilitative Services
2811-A Industrial Plaza
Tallahassee, FL 32301
(904) 488-4900

GEORGIA
Office of Regulatory Services
Child Care Licensing Section
Department of Human Resources
2 Peach Street NW, 20th Floor
Atlanta, GA 30303-3167
(404) 657-5562

HAWAII
Licensing and Registration Unit
Department of Human Services
33 S. King Street, Suite 500
Honolulu, HI 96813
(808) 586-7090

IDAHO
Day Care Licensing
Bureau of Social Services
Department of Health and Welfare
450 W. State Street, 3rd Floor
Boise, ID 83720-5450
(208) 334-5700

ILLINOIS
Home Day Care:
Day Care Unit
Department of Children and
    Family Services
406 East Monroe
Springfield, IL 62701-1498
(217) 785-2598

Day Care Centers:
Day Care Licensing
Children's Services Division
Department of Human Services
510 North Pestigo Court
Chicago, IL 60611
(312) 744-7828

INDIANA
Day Care Licensing
Child Welfare and Social
    Services Division
402 W. Washington Street,
Room W-364
Indianapolis, IN 46204
(317) 232-4521

IOWA
Day Care Unit
Department of Human Services
Bureau of Adult, Children, and
    Family Services
Hoover State Office Building,
    5th Floor
Des Moines, IA 50319
(515) 281-6074

KANSAS
Child Care Licensing and
    Registration
Department of Health and
    Environment
Mills Building
109 SW 9th Street, Suite 400-C
Topeka, KS 66612-2217
(913) 296-1272

KENTUCKY
Licensing and Regulation
Day Care Unit
Human Resources Office
Fourth Floor East
275 East Main Street
Frankfort, KY 40621
(502) 564-2800

LOUISIANA
Department of Social Services
License Bureau
Day Care Unit
P.O. Box 3078
Baton Rouge, LA 70821
(504) 922-0015

MAINE
Licensing Unit/Day Care
Department of Human Services
221 State Street
State House Station 11
Augusta, ME 04333
(207) 287-5060

MARYLAND
Child Care Administration
Department of Human Resources
2701 N. Charles Street
Baltimore, MD 21218
(410) 767-7063

MASSACHUSETTS
Day Care Licensing
Office of Children
1 Ashburton Place, 11th Floor
Boston, MA 02108
(617) 727-8900

MICHIGAN
Office of Day Care Licensing
Department of Social Services
335 South Grand Avenue, Suite 1208
P.O. Box 30037
Lansing, MI 48909
(517) 373-8300

MINNESOTA
Division of Licensing
Department of Human Services
444 Lafayette Road, 6th Floor
St. Paul, MN 55101
(612) 296-3768

MISSISSIPPI
Child Care Licensing Division
Department of Health
P.O. Box 1700
Jackson, MS 39215-1700
(601) 960-7613

MISSOURI
Day Care Licensing
Division of Family Services
P.O. Box 570
Jefferson City, MO 65102
(314) 751-2450

MONTANA
Child Care Licensing
Department of Family Services
P.O. Box 8005
Helena, MT 59604
(406) 444-5900

NEBRASKA
Day Care Licensing
Department of Social Services
P.O. Box 95026
Lincoln, NE 68509-5026
(402) 471-9302

NEVADA
Day Care Licensing
Department of Human Resources
Bureau of Services for Child Care
711 East 5th Street
Carson City, NV 89710
(702) 687-5982

NEW HAMPSHIRE
Department of Health and
    Human Services
Child Care Licensing
Division of Public Health Services
6 Hazen Drive
Concord, NH 00301-6527
(603) 271-4624

NEW JERSEY
Day Care Unit
Bureau of Licensing
Division of Youth and
    Family Services
CN-717
Trenton, NJ 08625-0717
(609) 292-1018

NEW MEXICO
Day Care Unit
Licensing and Certification Bureau
Public Health Division
P.O. Box 26110
Santa Fe, NM 87502-6110
(505) 827-2551

NEW YORK STATE
Department of Social Services
Day Care Licensing Unit
40 North Pearl St. (330 Broadway)
Albany, NY 12243
(518) 432-2763

NEW YORK CITY
Division of Day Care
Department of Health
65 Worth Street
New York, NY 10013
(212) 334-7814

NORTH CAROLINA
Division of Child Development
Department of Human Resources
P.O. Box 29553
Raleigh, NC 27626-0553
(919) 733-4801

NORTH DAKOTA
Office of Children and
    Family Services
Department of Human Services
State Capitol Building
600 East Boulevard Avenue
Bismarck, ND 58505
(701) 224-2316

OHIO
Child Day Care Licensing Section
Bureau of Child Care Services
65 East State Street, 5th Floor
Columbus, OH 43215
(614) 466-3822

OKLAHOMA
Office of Child Care
Department of Human Services
4545 N. Lincoln, Suite 100
Oklahoma City, OK 73105
(405) 521-3561

OREGON
Day Care Unit
Children's Services Division
Department of Human Resources
875 Union St. NE
Salem, OR 97311
(503) 378-3178

PENNSYLVANIA
Bureau of Child Day Care Services
P.O. Box 2675
Harrisburg, PA 17105-2675
(717) 787-8691

RHODE ISLAND
Day Care Licensing Unit
Department for Children and
    Their Families
10 Stable Square
Providence, RI 02903
(401) 457-4580

SOUTH CAROLINA
Division of Child Day Care Licensing
    and Regulatory Services
P.O. Box 1520
Columbia, SC 29202
(803) 734-5740

SOUTH DAKOTA
Child Protection Office
Department of Social Services
Kneip Building
700 Governors Drive
Pierre, SD 57501-2291
(605) 773-3227

TENNESSEE
Department of Human Services
Day Care Licensing Division
400 Deaderick Street
Citizen Plaza Building
Nashville, TN 37248-9800
(615) 741-7129

TEXAS
Department of Human Services
10205 N. Lamar Street
Austin, TX 78761
(512) 834-0162

UTAH
Office of Licensing
Department of Human Services
P.O. Box 45500
Salt Lake City, UT 84145-0500
(801) 538-4242

VERMONT
Children's Day Care Unit
Department of Social and
    Rehabilitation Services
103 South Main Street
Waterbury, VT 05671-2401
(802) 241-2158

VIRGINIA
Day Care Unit
Division of Service Programs
730 East Broad Street
Theatre Row
Richmond, VA 23219-1849
(804) 692-1298

WASHINGTON
Day Care Unit
P.O. Box 45710
Division of Children and
    Family Services
Department of Social and
    Health Services
Olympia, WA 98504
(206) 753-7002

WEST VIRGINIA
Day Care Licensing Unit
Office of Social Services
Capitol Complex
Building 6, Room 850
Charleston, WV 25305
(304) 558-7980

WISCONSIN
Bureau for Children, Youth and
    Families
Department of Health and Social
    Services
P.O. Box 7851
Madison, WI 53707-7851
(608) 266-8200

WYOMING
Child Care Unit
Department of Family Services
2300 Capital Avenue
Hathaway Building, 3rd Floor
Cheyenne, WY 82002
(307) 777-6595

CHAPTER 8

CHILDREN AND TAXES

Preparing for April 15

NUTS AND BOLTS

Is it a boy? Is it a girl? It makes no difference to Uncle Sam: he treats every baby the same. Instead of presenting parents with a silver baby cup or a teething ring to celebrate the birth, Uncle Sam gives all new parents a more lucrative gift: a tax deduction good for 18 years (or longer for some parents).

There's more to understanding the tax consequences of having a baby than claiming an additional dependent on your income tax return. And the more you know about how the tax laws affect you and your children, the less you'll have to pay in taxes and the better the financial decisions you'll be able to make for your family.

FILING FOR PARENTS

When you send out birth announcements, you may want to send one to the Internal Revenue Service signed "and many happy (tax) returns." In addition to being a source of great joy, your children can also be a source of terrific tax deductions and credits. As a parent you may be able to claim your child as a dependent, you may be able to claim your child's medical expenses as a deduction, and you may qualify for a child-care tax credit if you spend money to have someone watch your child while you work.

Claiming Your Child as a Dependent

While some parents strive to have their children born at the stroke of midnight on January 1, Baby New Year isn't worth a dime as a tax deduction. You can only claim a deduction for a child born during the calendar year. How much is your new family member worth to the Internal Revenue Service? In 1993, $2,350 as a personal exemption.

On your tax return you can claim a personal exemption for yourself, your spouse, and each dependent child. The personal exemption is an amount that you may deduct from your income before computing your tax.

In order to claim an exemption for your child or any other dependent, you must satisfy the five following tests:

- **Gross income test**. This test doesn't apply to your children under age 19 or full-time students under age 24; dependent children over age 19 must have less than $2,350 of gross income in 1993.
- **Member of household or relationship test**. Of course, your children pass the IRS's relationship test. So do stepchildren, adopted children, and foster children, or other relatives if they live with you for the year.
- **Support test**. You must provide more than half of your dependent's total support. If parents divorce, only one parent—usually the parent who has custody—can claim the child as a dependent and receive the deduction.
- **Citizenship test**. Your dependent must be a citizen or resident of the United States or a resident of Canada or Mexico.
- **Joint return test**. Your dependent can't file a joint return unless it was filed solely to claim a refund. For example, if you had a grown child who was married and filed a joint return, you could not claim that child as a dependent even if you provided financial support.

Tax exemptions—even those for infant children—aren't absolute. The value of the personal exemption is phased out for high-income families. The more money you make, the less valuable your personal exemptions become. You must reduce the amount of your exemption by 2 percent for each $2,500 that your adjusted gross income exceeds certain limits. In 1992, for example, if you were married and filing jointly, the phaseout began when your adjusted gross income reached $157,900.

Claiming Your Medical Expenses as a Deduction

You may deduct medical and dental expenses for yourself, your spouse, your children, and your other dependents—but you'll have to face a whopping medical bill to qualify. First you must subtract from the total payments the amount of any insurance or other reimbursements you have received. Then, you can deduct only the net medical expenses that exceed 7.5 percent of your adjusted gross income. Your adjusted gross income is the total of all your income, minus your deductions. For example, if your adjusted gross income were $50,000, you'd have to have unreimbursed medical bills in excess of $3,750 to qualify for a deduction, and then you'd only be allowed to deduct the amount over $3,750.

The IRS is a bit more liberal in defining dependents when it comes to medical expenses than it is when it comes to personal exemptions. When calculating medical deductions, the term dependent includes not only anyone you have actually claimed as a dependent but also any person you could have claimed had he or she not had gross income of $2,300 or more or filed a joint return.

In the case of a child of divorced parents the deduction goes to the parent who actually paid for the child's medical care. If both parents chipped in, each parent can deduct only the amount he or she actually paid.

What qualifies as a medical expense? Many of the costs you would expect: prescription drugs and medicines, doctors' fees, hospital expenses, medical insurance premiums (including those withheld from your paycheck by your employer), medical supplies and equipment, care of the handicapped, and alcoholism and drug abuse treatment. The list of qualified expenses also includes some services one might not expect, such as legal abortion, acupuncture, birth-control pills, child-birth preparation classes, guide dogs, and contact lenses. The IRS says no to cosmetic surgery (unless it's to treat illness or disease), exercise and weight-loss programs, and smoking-cessation classes. (See the Resources section for information on obtaining the free IRS publication listing qualified expenses.)

Child-Care Tax Credits

If you pay someone to take care of your dependent children (under age 13) while you work, you may be entitled to claim a child-care credit against your tax. (You can also claim the credit for care of your spouse, a parent, or any other dependent incapable of caring for himself or herself.) Keep in mind that tax credits are more valuable than deductions: instead of merely reducing the amount of income you must pay tax on, tax credits offset dollar for dollar the amount of tax you owe.

If you are married, you and your spouse must both work full or part time to qualify for the child-care tax credit. The expenses that qualify include child care and household services that benefit the child or qualified dependent. Transportation costs to and from day care don't qualify. Since the tax credit is intended to help families in which the parents work outside the home, it doesn't apply to child-care expenses incurred while parents aren't working. For example, expenses of attending a daytime summer camp while parents work would qualify, but overnight camp expenses would not—not even the portion that covers the daytime.

Calculating the credit can be a bit tricky. The credit is allowed for a percentage of up to $2,400 of expenses for one child and $4,800 for two or more. That doesn't mean you get a tax credit of $2,400 or a $4,800 credit: your credit is equal to between 20 and 30 percent of that amount.

The percentage you're entitled to use depends on your adjusted gross income. If your adjusted gross income is $10,000 or less, you can claim the 30 percent credit; if your adjusted gross income exceeds $28,000, you can claim only 20 percent of the qualified expenses as a credit. If your adjusted gross income falls between those two extremes, the 30 percent credit is cut by 1 percent for each $2,000 in adjusted gross income in excess of $10,000. The lower your adjusted gross income, the higher the percentage you can claim.

For example, if you spend $4,800 in qualified expenses for two children and your adjusted gross income is $10,000 or less, you qualify for the maximum credit of $1,440 (30 percent of $4,800). If you spent the same amount for two children but your adjusted gross income was $28,000, your credit would be $960 (20 percent of $4,800).

In order to claim the credit you must include the name, address, and taxpayer identification number of your child-care provider on your tax return. This is a way the IRS has of checking up on you: If you claim the credit, the IRS will catch you if you aren't paying Social Security and other taxes for your employee. If you have an au pair, you can claim the credit for the portion of the money spent on child care but not the compensation for housekeeping, cooking, and other chores, if any.

Another restriction on claiming the credit: Your day-care center must meet applicable state laws (such as licensing laws and fire code regulations) if the facility provides care for more than six children. If the facility deals with six or fewer children, you can claim the credit whether or not the standards are met.

FILING FOR YOUR KIDS

Before 1986 things were simple: you provided food and shelter for your kids, and they provided a tidy tax shelter for you in exchange. But those days are gone. Many children must now file tax returns on money earning interest in their names.

The requirements for paying tax on your children's income can be quite confusing. Your child may have to file a tax return if he or she has income, whether earned income (for example, modeling fees for a small child or wages from a summer job for an older child) or unearned income (interest, dividends, royalties, and other investment income).

Unearned Income. According to the IRS, unearned income includes any money not received as wages or compensation for a job. Unearned income includes interest on investments; gifts of cash, stocks, or bonds; prize money; scholarship money; and Social Security survivor's benefits.

If your child collects less than $600 in unearned income, he or she owes no taxes and doesn't need to file a tax return. If your child collects between $600 and $1,200 in unearned income, he or she must pay tax at his or her marginal tax rate (probably 15 percent).

If your child collects more than $1,200 in unearned income and is under age 14, he or she must pay taxes at the family's maximum marginal tax rate. This so-called kiddie tax is designed to discourage people from sheltering income-producing property by transferring it to their young children.

The rules change when your child reaches 14 (as the parent of any adolescent knows). As with younger children, the first $600 of unearned income is tax-free, but with children 14 and older, *any* income above that amount is taxed at the child's rate, probably 15 percent. (In 1993 your child would have to collect an additional $22,100 in unearned income to be pushed to the 28 percent marginal tax bracket.)

From the government's point of view it doesn't matter when during the year your child turns 14. In other words, your child is taxed as a 14-year-old all year even if his or her birthday falls on December 31.

In most cases, if your child owes tax on unearned income, you may report your child's unearned income on your return to avoid filing separately for your child. To do so you must file Form 8814, Parent's Election to Report Child's Interest and Dividends, with your own 1040. You and your child must meet certain requirements, however. Your child must be under 14 years of age, and the child's unearned gross income must be more than $600 but less than $5,000.

Earned Income. You probably won't have to worry about paying taxes on earned income until your child becomes old enough to hold a summer job (unless, of course, your baby is recruited to be the Gerber model). In such a case, if your child has gross income—a combination of earned and unearned income—greater than the standard deduction, he or she must file. Defining the standard deduction can be confusing. In 1992 the standard deduction was defined as either $600 or the amount of the child's earned income, up to a limit of $3,600. When calculating your child's tax liability, remember that your child cannot claim a personal exemption as long as he or she is claimed as a dependent on your tax return. No double dipping allowed.

In addition to tax considerations you may want to work with your wage-earning child to establish good budgeting and money management skills. For more information see Chapter 9.

UNDER AGE 14

If your child receives...	Your child pays...
Less than $600 in unearned income	No tax and doesn't need to file a tax return.
More than $600 but less than $1,200	At the child's marginal rate of 15 percent.
More than $1,200	At the family's marginal tax rate.

OVER AGE 14

If your child receives...	Your child pays...
Less than $600 in unearned income	No tax and doesn't need to file a tax return.
More than $600	At the child's marginal rate of 15 percent.

ISSUES TO DISCUSS:
WHAT PARENTS SHOULD TALK ABOUT

- ☐ Do we have enough medical expenses to itemize our deductions?
- ☐ Do our child-care arrangements allow us to take advantage of the child-care tax credit?
- ☐ Do we need to file a tax return for our child?
- ☐ Are our finances set up to maximize the tax advantages for our children under age 14? Over age 14?
- ☐ Have we filed the necessary paperwork for our household employees? (See Chapter 7.)

QUESTIONS & ANSWERS

Can I claim my unborn child as a dependent?

Not until he or she is born. Though religious scholars and the U.S. Supreme Court may debate whether life begins at conception, the Internal Revenue Service has declared that deductions begin at birth.

I have not yet legally adopted my child, though she is living with me. Can I claim a deduction?

Yes, if the child has been placed with you by an adoption agency and is living as a member of your household. You can claim the full deduction even if the child has not been with you for the entire year.

My child died several days after he was born. Can I claim a deduction?

Yes, but if he had been stillborn, you would not have been able to claim the deduction. You must have proof of a live birth, such as a birth certificate.

My ex-husband and I have joint custody of our children. Which one of us can claim the tax deduction?

To the IRS there is no such thing as truly joint custody. One parent does more for the child and that parent is eligible to take the deduction. First the IRS looks to the divorce decree to determine the primary parent. If the decree isn't explicit, the next issue under consideration is residence. If a child does split six months with each parent, the next issue is money spent to support the child. Ultimately the parents must resolve the issue. If both try to claim the deduction, both deductions will be disallowed. One notable exception to the general rule: The noncustodial parent may be allowed the deduction under certain decrees of divorce and separate maintenance agreements executed before January 1, 1985. If such an agreement exists and the noncustodial parent has provided at least $600 for the child's support, the noncustodial parent should check the "pre-1985 agreement" box on his or her Form 1040.

Can I claim a medical deduction for the cost of childbirth classes?

Yes, you can deduct the portion of the expenses for attending childbirth classes that covers the actual instruction in birthing techniques and other preparation for labor and delivery. You cannot deduct the cost of classes that cover the baby's growth and development, though they are beneficial to your understanding of the baby's overall health and well-being.

Can I deduct the cost of maternity clothes?

Nope. While any pregnant woman knows that finding maternity clothes that fit and are flattering can be a federal case, the IRS considers it a personal matter—and not worthy of a deduction.

This child will be our last. My husband is planning to have a vasectomy. Is this a deductible medical expense or a personal expense?

The costs of birth control pills, abortions, vasectomies, and operations for sterilizations have all been ruled deductible.

My ex-husband and I are in different tax brackets. Our daughter will have to pay tax, but whose rate applies?

Your daughter should pay tax at the rate of the parent who has custody. If you and your ex-husband have joint custody, the rate is that of the parent with the higher rate—just as it would be if you were married and filed separate returns. In a case where both parents are deceased, a child pays taxes at his or her own rate.

I do volunteer work and my husband works for pay. Does the baby-sitter I hire when I go to "work" qualify for the child-care credit?

No. Volunteer work—or near-volunteer work, for which you receive a nominal salary—doesn't satisfy the requirement. The only time both spouses don't need to be working for pay to qualify for the child-care credit is when one is a full-time student or is physically or mentally incapable of taking care of himself or herself.

I want to hire my 16-year-old daughter to baby-sit my three-month-old son while I go to work. Can I claim the child-care credit?

No. You can't claim the child-care tax credit for payments made to children under age 19 or a person who qualifies as a dependent of you or your spouse. Try again when your daughter is 19 and she is sitting for her three-year-old brother. (But keep in mind that you'll have to pay taxes and Social Security for her.)

What is a dependent-care flexible spending account?

It's a benefit offered by some employers that allows you to receive tax-free reimbursement for child-care expenses that allow you to work. You can contribute up to $5,000 of your salary per year to the plan ($2,500 if you are married and you file a separate tax return). The payment may be made only for expenses that, if you paid them directly, would qualify for the child-care tax credit. If you participate in the plan, the child-care benefits you receive aren't subject to Social Security or federal employment tax.

Last year I did not claim a medical expense that I have since learned would have been allowed. What can I do?

You can't just claim the deduction on this year's tax return; you must file an amended return. File Form 1040X, Amended U.S. Individual Income Tax Return, for the year you should have claimed the deduction. Your amended returns must be filed within three years from the date the original return was filed.

I seem to have misplaced my tax returns from the past several years. Where can I get copies of the returns?

From the IRS, of course. You can get copies of past returns by filling out Form 4506, Request for Copy of Tax Form, and paying a small fee. If all you need is a specific piece of information—such as the amount of your reported income or the total amount of tax you owed—you may be able to get the information free by calling the IRS at (800) 829-1040.

I hired a nanny through an agency. Do I have to pay Social Security and employment taxes?

If a placement agency sets the fee and controls the nanny by establishing rules of conduct and requiring periodic reports, then the nanny is working for the agency, not for you, even if you pay the nanny directly. If, however, the agency gave you a list of nannies and you chose one, then you're the boss—and you need to file taxes.

STEP BY STEP: PREPARING FOR APRIL 15

- Buy or borrow from the library a good, clear tax preparation book. Read every section that applies to children and filing tax returns for your children, since the tax laws are forever changing.
- Review your medical expenses to see whether they qualify for an itemized deduction.
- If both parents work outside the home and pay for child-care services, assess how much of a child-care tax credit you qualify for.
- If your child has unearned income, review to see whether you need to file a tax return in his or her name.
- Consider meeting with a financial planner or tax adviser to see if you are taking maximum advantage of investments for your children.

RESOURCES:
WHERE TO GO FOR MORE INFORMATION

BOOKS

■ **Guide to Income Tax Preparation**, by Warren H. Esanu, Barry Dickman, Elias Zuckerman, Michael Pollet, and the Editors of Consumer Reports Books. Cost: $13.95, plus $2.50 shipping and handling. Contact: Consumer Reports, 9180 LeSaint Drive, Fairfield, OH 45014; (513) 860-1178

■ **The Price Waterhouse Personal Tax Adviser**. Cost: $9.95. Contact: Pocket Books, Order Processing Center, P.O. Box 11071, Des Moines, IA 50336-1071; (800) 947-7700, (212) 698-7000.

BROCHURES

■ The Internal Revenue Service offers a series of publications on tax matters, including:

"Your Rights as a Taxpayer" (Publication 1)
"Your Federal Income Tax" (Publication 17)

"Exemptions, Standard Deduction, and Filing Information" (Publication 501)

"Medical and Dental Expenses" (Publication 502)

"Child and Dependent Care Credit" (Publication 503)

"Tax Information for Divorced and Separated Individuals" (Publication 504)

"Educational Expenses" (Publication 508)

"Scholarships and Fellowships" (Publication 520)

"Employment Taxes for Household Employers" (Publication 926)

All of these publications are available free from the Internal Revenue Service, (800) 829-3676.

ORGANIZATIONS

- **The Internal Revenue Service** operates a staffed tax hotline at (800) 829-1040.

GLOSSARY: UNDERSTANDING THE TERMS

Adjusted gross income: Your total income, minus your allowable deductions and credits.

Marginal tax rate: The tax rate as established by law on your last dollar of earnings.

Tax liability: The amount of tax you owe.

Unearned income: Income from sources other than wages, salaries, tips, and other forms of compensation. For example, unearned income includes income from interest, dividends, royalties, and other investment income. It also includes gifts, prize money, scholarships, and Social Security survivor's benefits.

CHAPTER 9

ECONOMICS 101

Saving for Your Child's College Education

NUTS AND BOLTS

Unless you are very rich or very poor, you'd better plan ahead if you want to be ready when it's time to send your child to college. If you haven't considered the cost of college in the twenty-first century, prepare yourself for tuition sticker shock. Sending a child to four years at a private university is one of the most costly investments most families ever make. For many parents a college education costs more than any other family purchase, except a house. And if you have two children, you'll have to do all this saving, times two.

If your child is young, time is on your side. You can take advantage of long-term savings—and the miracle of compounding interest—by beginning to invest in the college fund *now*. One of the biggest and most common financial errors that young parents make is their failure to plan ahead for their children's education.

The earlier you begin to save, the easier it will be to reach your savings goals. As you will see, there are a number of different ways to save for college, but every method starts with making a commitment to save. You don't have to try to finance the entire amount right away; just get into the habit of setting some amount—even just $10 or $20 a month—aside for college. Treat your deposits in the college account as a regular monthly expense, not something you choose to do with the money left over after all the bills are paid. You'll be surprised at how much you can save over the next 18 to 20 years by simply getting into a savings routine.

Of course, saving is a sacrifice. Money earmarked for the college fund can't be spent on family trips to Disney World or other tempting indulgences, but it may help to think of college as an investment in your child's future. And it is. Studies show that college graduates earn about $600,000 more over their lifetimes than those who close the books after earning a high school diploma. And no price can be assigned to the personal benefits and broader outlook on life provided by an advanced education.

IN YOUR BEST INTEREST

Save early, save often. That's the key to easing the financial burden of saving for college. Yes, one type of investment may do better than another in the long term, but doing something is always better than doing nothing. For example, if you deposited just $10 per week in an investment or an account earning 8 percent interest, over a period of 18 years your investment would grow to $20,993. Not bad.

The secret is compounding interest. If you make an investment and allow the interest to accumulate, you will soon be earning interest on interest. Compounding interest can have a dramatic impact on your long-term investments.

How long will it take to reach your savings goals? If you want a general idea without breaking out the calculator or math program on your personal computer, you can use the rule of 72 to find out how long it will take to double your money. Simply divide the interest rate you are collecting on your investment into 72 and the answer is a rough approximation of how long it will take to double your money. For example, if you can get a 9 percent return on your money in a certain investment, then your money will double every eight years (72 divided by 9 equals 8). If your investment yields only 6 percent, then it will take 12 years.

These days savings entails more than just making a deposit into a regular savings account. You have to invest your savings wisely. When

TIMING IS EVERYTHING

As the following table shows, money you invest in the college fund in the early years goes much further than dollars invested later on. The calculations are based on investments earning 7 percent interest, compounded monthly.

Preschool Savings		High School Savings	
Amount Saved Each Year for 4 Years*	Value When Child Is Ready for College	Amount Saved Each Year for 4 Years	Value When Child Is Ready for College
$1,000	$12,224	$1,000	$4,601
$5,000	$61,116	$5,000	$23,003
$10,000	$122,238	$10,000	$46,008
$15,000	$183,357	$15,000	$69,012

*Assumes no additional payments are made for the next 14 years.

considering various investment options, you must remember that while interest is increasing the value of your money, inflation is eroding it. Money stashed in the proverbial cookie jar isn't earning interest; it will be worth less a year from now because inflation will have nibbled at its earning potential. Inflation makes saving for college particularly challenging because during the last decade or so college costs have increased faster than the rate of inflation. Parents have to plan carefully to maximize their savings.

INVESTING IN THE FUTURE

It's impossible to know how much college will cost by the time your newborn is ready to head off for freshman orientation. The tuition bill you and your spouse will be facing depends on whether your child attends a public or a private school, whether he or she commutes from home or lives away at school, and just how much college costs increase in the next 18 years. As the table on page 178 shows, the costs can be almost three times higher than today's rates.

Don't become overwhelmed by the big picture. You want to save as much as possible, but many parents don't want to save the entire

KIDS AND MONEY

As they grow up, your children are going to reflect your attitudes about money. If you're frugal and careful with a dollar, your children will learn thrift; if you're a spendthrift who buys things to make yourself feel good, your children will learn little about delayed gratification and financial planning. It's up to you to decide what values and attitudes you want your children to have about money.

Start with an allowance—a good foundation for your children to develop a basic understanding of money and how it works. In deciding how much allowance to give your child, make sure it's enough to cover the basic expenses, with a little something left over to save or squander. A preschooler's allowance can be a nominal amount—say, 50 cents a week. It should be sufficient to cover the costs of candy or a comic book, enough to teach the idea of money in exchange for goods and services.

In elementary school, kids should get a raise. But with the increase in income should come an increase in responsibility to pay for friends' gifts, hobby supplies, and other nonessential items. You probably don't want to give your child a budget that includes money for school clothes or books, though, since many children will blow the money on other items and neither one of you will be happy with the consequences. Most grade-school-age kids aren't ready to handle a lot of money.

At this age you may want to introduce the concept of working for money by allowing your child to perform extra chores to earn extra money. It's best to separate allowance from routine household chores, however, because you don't want to raise a mercenary monster who will work only if there's money involved. It's important for children to learn that we all have certain chores and responsibilities simply because we are part of a family.

During the teen years you can go a long way toward preparing your child for financial adulthood by working together to form a budget. You might want to work out a comprehensive budget, including money for social activities, food, school activities, and other items. Again, you want to make sure to give your child enough money so that if he or she spends wisely, there will be enough money to make it through the month, but not so much that there won't be choices to make. A tight budget can help a child learn to comparison-shop and to save for long-term expenses. If your child wants a pair of $100 tennis shoes that you don't want to pay for, you might agree to pay $50 or whatever you would pay for regular shoes and allow your child to come up with the rest.

If your child comes into a considerable amount of money, either through a job, an inheritance, or a gift from relatives, it's even more important to work with the child to develop a budget. The overall plan should include money to spend now, money to save for a longer-term goal, general savings, and college savings.

Tips to Help Teach Frugality and Thrift

- Offer to match savings dollar for dollar. (This could be especially important for money deposited in the college fund.)

- Help your child complain to the Better Business Bureau, state attorney general, or consumer organizations about product misrepresentation or faulty products.

- Allow your teenage child to use a supplemental card issued on your MasterCard or Visa account. Limit the purchases and require your child to pay the interest and a portion of the annual fee. Explain to your son or daughter the difference between different credit cards and the importance of comparing a card's interest rate, annual fee, and grace period before interest is charged on purchases.

- When it's time to pay the bills, sit down with your teen and show how much the electric, water, and other utilities cost each month. (This might even help your child understand the importance of turning off the lights when leaving a room.)

- When April 15 rolls around, take time to show your child how to fill out a tax form and explain the various tax brackets. If you're comfortable doing so, you may want to review your tax return with your child, pointing out the portion of income that goes into federal, state, and local taxes. This will show your child the very real difference between gross pay and take-home pay.

- You might consider allowing your teenager to borrow money—$100 or so—from you, with interest. Draw up a contract and have your child make monthly payments.

HOW MUCH WILL COLLEGE COST IN 2015?

The costs may seem astronomical, but you can afford to send your child to college. You may have to scrimp and save, borrow, and apply for financial aid, but you can find a way to pay for higher education if you set your mind to it.

College costs have skyrocketed since 1980. During the 1980s tuition and fees rose an average of 9 percent a year at state colleges and nearly 10 percent at private schools. If that rate of increase continues, a bachelor's degree for a baby born in the 1990s will cost between $100,000 and $300,000—or even more.

Don't give up. Work out a savings plan and follow it. Self-reliance is key: While you should make yourself familiar with the financial aid offerings, you can't be sure those programs will be around 18 years from now.

The following chart may give you some idea of the impact of a relatively modest 7 percent educational inflation factor:

Four-Year Costs, Including Room and Board

Year Entering	Public College or University	Private College or University	Exclusive Private College or University
1993	$27,400	$69,800	$98,500
1994	29,592	75,384	106,380
1995	31,959	81,415	114,890
1996	34,516	87,928	124,082
1997	37,277	94,962	134,008
1998	40,260	102,559	144,729
1999	43,480	110,764	156,307
2000	46,959	119,625	168,812
2001	50,715	129,195	182,317
2002	54,773	139,531	196,902
2003	59,155	150,693	212,654
2004	63,887	162,748	229,666
2005	68,998	175,768	248,040
2006	74,518	189,830	267,883
2007	80,479	205,016	289,314
2008	86,917	221,417	312,459
2009	93,871	239,131	337,455
2010	101,380	258,261	364,452
2011	109,491	278,922	393,608
2012	118,250	301,236	459,104
2013	127,710	325,335	495,833
2014	137,927	351,362	535,499
2015	148,961	379,471	578,339

amount anyway. Some parents want to share the burden with their children by asking them to chip in with money from summer jobs, scholarships, or work-study jobs. (See box, "Kids and Money," on page 176.)

In addition most families pay for college from a variety of sources, not just the college fund. Most parents finance college with a combination of money saved for college, money borrowed to pay for college, and financial aid. You don't have to do it all yourself, but it's wise to save as much as possible since you can't be sure what kind of financial aid packages will be available in the year 2015.

When it comes to selecting investments for the college fund, the general rule is: The closer your child is to college, the more conservative your investments should be. In fact, many financial planners recommend that parents begin to switch funds from stock mutual funds and other somewhat higher-risk investments to the more secure (and less lucrative) bond funds and other predictable investments when their children enter high school.

Your investment strategy depends on your personality and your willingness to accept risk. Some parents are willing to put their money in investments that could go belly up in exchange for the possibility of greater growth or return on their money over the long haul. For example, if they invest their money in a new company that goes bankrupt, their money is gone; however, if that company proves to be the next Microsoft, then the company prospers and so do the parents. In the end parents have to balance their desire for a greater return on their money with their desire for stability and security. Unfortunately you can't have it all: The greater the possible return, the greater the risk of losing some or all of the money invested.

In planning a savings strategy, also consider your child's age. As discussed in Chapter 8, if your child is under age 14, interest earned on investments held in your child's name will be taxed at your rate after the first $1,200. After age 14 the investment income is taxed at the child's rate. Some parents try to minimize the tax bite by looking for long-term investments that don't pay out until after the child turns 14, so the interest will be taxed at the child's marginal tax rate.

There is no single best way to save for college. If you went to five different financial planners, you'd probably receive five different college savings plans. For this reason be careful when you solicit financial advice. (For additional information on selecting a financial planner, see the box on page 184.)

While the following list is by no means comprehensive, it provides a brief summary of some of the most popular investment options for the college fund:

Bonds

Bonds are basically IOUs. A corporation, government body, or municipality issues a bond and promises to repay the borrowed money at a fixed rate of interest. Bonds provide a good, stable investment for the college fund because you know exactly how much your money will be worth when the bond matures. If you want to have $25,000 in the college fund to cover tuition in the year 2012, you can buy enough bonds to produce the exact yield you want in the year you want it.

IN WHOSE NAME?

The decision of whether to keep investments in accounts in your name or your child's can be a tricky one. It depends on several factors, most importantly the tax consequences, the financial aid consequences, and the consequences of handing over a significant amount of money to an 18-year-old.

• **Taxes**. If taxes are your primary concern, put the funds in the child's name. As discussed in Chapter 8, if the money is invested in the child's name, then up to $600 of investment income will be tax-free each year and another $600 will be taxed at the child's marginal tax rate. Additional income will be taxed at the parents' rate until the year the child reaches 14. And that year and thereafter, the child's rate is used for all income. Assuming your child's tax rate is 15 percent, the tax bill on the first $1,200 of interest, dividends, or capital gains would be $90. If that $1,200 was your income and taxed at the 28 percent bracket, the tab would be $336.

• **Financial Aid**. If qualifying for financial aid is your primary concern, keep the funds in your name. When it comes to calculating the amount of financial aid a student will receive, it is assumed that 70 percent of the student's income and 35 percent of the student's savings are available for school but only 47 percent of the parents' income and about 6 percent of the parents' savings.

• **Control**. If you want to make sure the money you've saved for college is spent on college, you'll have to control the purse strings yourself. Money invested in the child's name belongs to the child once he or she reaches age 18. If your child decides to withdraw the money, buy a Porsche, and drive from coast to coast, there's nothing you can do about it once the child reaches majority age.

Some parents try to move the money around to take advantage of each situation. To maximize the tax advantages, for children under age 14 you could invest in the child's name that amount of money that would earn up to $1,200 interest (after that interest is taxed at Mom and Dad's rate). Then the money can be saved in your account, since you'd have to pay tax on it at your rate anyway.

For children age 14 to 18 you might want to shift money into the child's account for several years since it will be taxed at the child's rate instead of your rate. But you'll want to transfer it back to your account the year before applying for financial aid so that you can qualify for the maximum amount.

If you plan to switch the funds around, don't set up an account using the Uniform Gift to Minors Act (UGMA) (see Chapter 1). Such accounts are easy to set up and an excellent vehicle for a college savings fund, but the funds are irrevocable: once you give the money to your child, you can't take it back or restrict how it's spent.

Everything's under control, right? Not entirely. The downside is that inflation can eat away at the value of your investment. If interest rates go up, you might be able to earn more money on some other type of investment than on bonds, but your money is already locked into this long-term commitment. Of course, you can sell your bonds on the secondary market, but you'd probably take a financial beating. If you bought a bond at 7 percent and interest rates climbed to 12 percent, why would someone want to buy your bond when that person could buy a current bond that offers a higher rate of return?

Because of this trade-off between predictability and the threat of inflation, many people include bonds as part, but not all, of the college fund. There are a number of different types of bonds:

■ **Series EE Bonds**. These bonds make sense for parents who want to minimize risk. Series EE bonds are fully insured U.S. government bonds sold in denominations ranging from $50 to $10,000; they are sold for half their face value (a $100 bond costs $50 to purchase). The government limits the amount that can be purchased to $15,000 annually ($30,000 face value) per person, per year. If you co-own a bond with a child, you can effectively double the limit.

One of the most important features of series EE bonds is that there is no tax due on accumulated interest until the bonds mature and are cashed in. They are exempt from state and local taxes, and they may be exempt from federal income tax if the money is used to pay tuition and fees at colleges, universities, or qualified technical schools during the year you redeem the bonds. In order for the bonds to be tax-free you have to meet several conditions, including:

- The bonds must have been bought after December 31, 1989;
- The buyer has to be 24 or older at the time of purchase and the bond must be in the parent's name;
- The money must be used to educate the bond owner's dependents or spouse, or the bond owner.

To qualify for a full tax exemption, your adjusted gross income—including all accumulated interest on the EE bonds redeemed—cannot exceed set limits established by the IRS. In 1993 the exemption declines on higher incomes and disappears at $98,250 (joint) and $60,500 (individual). The limits are adjusted yearly for inflation.

If your income is too high to qualify for the tax breaks, you may still be able to save by shifting the tax liability to your child by buying the bonds in his or her name. That way if you wait until the child is 14 or older to redeem the bond, the income will be taxed at the child's rate.

Series EE bonds can be purchased through most commercial banks, many savings institutions, and payroll savings plans offered by thousands of employers. Of course, you don't have to use the money for education. If you cash in the bond to finance a trip to Europe or a new car, the interest income won't be exempt from federal income tax, but you'll still enjoy the benefits of tax deferral and investment security.

The interest rates on series EE bonds change every year in October and April and are equal to 85 percent of the average yield on five-year Treasury securities. For information on rates call 1-800-4US-BOND.

■ **Municipal Bonds**. "Munis," or municipal bonds, make sense for many medium- and high-income families because they are free of federal, state, and local taxes. They tend to pay somewhat lower interest rates than other bonds, but for parents in higher-income tax brackets, the tax-free status may more than offset the lower yield. The bonds are usually issued by a city, county, or state government agency; they usually have maturities ranging from 10 to 40 years. If you consider including municipal bonds in your child's college fund, compare the interest rate with the after-tax rate of other investments.

■ **Zero-coupon Bonds**. Zero-coupon bonds pay no interest until the date they mature. One advantage of zeros is that you can invest for the long term with a relatively small amount of money: you buy the bonds at a deep discount from the $1,000 face amount of the bond. For example, a $1,000 zero-coupon bond paying 7 percent interest that matures in 14 years would cost about $382 in today's dollars.

The bonds have earned their name because you don't collect a penny on the bond in advance, though you are required to pay tax on the interest you earn each year just as if you had it to spend. For example, if you invested $10,000 in a zero-coupon bond that would be worth $50,000 in the year 2011, your investment would earn $40,000. You'd have to pay tax on that capital gain, but you wouldn't pay it in 2011, when you cashed in the bond to pay for college. Instead you'd pay a little bit every year, as though you had access to the cash.

It's possible to cash in a zero-coupon bond early, but as with other bonds, you'll usually lose money. You'll probably face stiff brokers' fees if you try to sell a bond before maturity. Zero-coupon bonds provide an excellent return in times when inflation is staying level and interest rates are steady or falling.

The most popular zero-coupon bonds are treasuries, which some brokerage firms package into financial products with strange names, such as TIGRS (treasury investment growth receipts), CATS (certificates of accrual on treasury securities), and STRIPS (separate trading of registered interest and principal of securities). The brokers' fees and other costs are folded into the price of the bonds, so shop around and compare yields. You can buy zeros from securities firms, discount brokers, and local banks.

CHOOSING THE RIGHT INVESTMENT HELP

A financial planner can help you develop a strategy for achieving your short- and long-term investment goals, including college financing. Most financial planners have training as accountants, lawyers, bankers, insurance agents, or stockbrokers. However, there are no statutory educational or professional requirements, testing programs, or licensing procedures for financial planners. Anyone can use the title "financial planner" no matter how much—or how little—training he or she has had.

When looking for a financial planner, consider the way the person is compensated:

• **Commissions-only planners** make their money on commissions on recommended investments, such as insurance policies, mutual funds, and other securities. You should be very cautious in following the advice of a commissions-only planner: they may try to steer you into high-priced, high-commission investments.

• **Fee-plus-commissions planners** charge an initial fee to draw up a master plan, then add commissions if investments are made through them. Some planners deduct the commissions from the original fee. Again, proceed with caution. Some of these planners steer clients toward high-commission products.

• **Fee-only planners** are the most expensive, but they are the only ones who have nothing at stake in the investment choice you make. Fees often range from $1,000 to $7,000 for the original plan, depending on the size and complexity of your assets. Others charge on an hourly basis.

• **Salaried planners** are paid directly by the banks, credit unions, and other organizations that hire them to provide financial advice to their members. When you are working with a salaried planner, make sure you feel confident that the planner is taking the appropriate time and collecting enough information to customize a plan to meet your needs. You don't want to work with someone who gives everyone the same advice. These planners may also have a bias toward investments offered by the groups paying their salaries. If you're not comfortable with their recommendations, talk to someone else before investing.

How to find a financial planner

More than 250,000 Americans call themselves financial planners, but fewer than one out of five of them has gone to the trouble of meeting the standards or requirements for certification by a professional organization or society.

Following is a list of several of the leading organizations of financial planners. On request each organization will provide a list of qualified member planners in your area. In addition you might want to talk with personal and professional contacts and ask for recommendations.

- **Institute of Certified Financial Planners**
  7600 East Eastman Avenue, Suite 301, Denver, CO 80231-4397
  (800) 282-7526, (303) 751-7600

Members earn the designation CFP.
Requirements: CFPs must complete a two-year, six-part program conducted by the College for Financial Planning; they must pass extensive tests, meet ethical standards set and enforced by the International Board of Standards and Practices for Certified Financial Planners, and take at least 30 hours of continuing education instruction every two years.

- **American Society of Charted Financial Consultants**
  American College, 270 Bryn Mawr Avenue, Bryn Mawr, PA 19010
  (610) 526-2500

Members earn the designation ChFC.
Requirements: ChFCs must have three years' experience in financial planning and pass 10 two-hour examinations.

- **International Association for Financial Planning**
  Two Concourse Parkway, Suite 800, Atlanta, GA 30328
  (404) 395-1605, (800) 945-4237

Members are eligible for referral from the Registry of Financial Planning Practitioners.
Requirements: Members of the registry must have a degree related to financial planning, three years' experience, and references from five clients. In addition members must pass a four-hour exam and participate in continuing education.

- **National Association of Personal Financial Advisors**
  1130 Lake Cook Road, Suite 150, Buffalo Grove, IL 60089
  (800) 366-2732, (708) 537-7722

Requirements: Members must be fee-only planners; they must have education related to financial planning and participate in continuing education.

■ **Baccalaureate Bonds**. About half the states have issued college savings bonds, sometimes called baccalaureate bonds, which come in maturities ranging from 5 to 21 years. These bonds sell at a large discount from their maturity value and pay no interest, but their face value increases from year to year. They are a type of municipal bond, meaning they are exempt from federal income tax and from state and local taxes, if you live in the state issuing the bond. They are typically issued in $1,000 units, and they allow parents to know how much money will be available when the child starts college. To find out whether your state has issued baccalaureate bonds, contact your state department of finance or a local brokerage firm.

■ **Other types of bonds**. Treasury bonds are what the U.S. government uses to finance the federal debt. The interest on these bonds is exempt from state and local tax. Treasury bonds are low risk, and therefore they pay the lowest interest rates. *Fannie Maes* and *federal home loan bank bonds* pay somewhat higher rates of interest, but they aren't fully insured. The minimum purchase ranges from $1,000 to $5,000, depending on the issuing agency. *Corporate bonds* pay still higher interest rates, but they are even riskier, and they are subject to federal, state, and local taxes. Holding a corporate bond isn't like holding stock: you don't own a piece of the company and you don't share in the profits; you're simply lending the company money at a fixed rate of interest. Corporate bonds fluctuate in value if they are sold before they mature. Corporate bonds are only as good as the company that issues them: you should check with a bond-rating service, such as Moody's Investors Services or Standard & Poor's, before purchasing them. (For details on assessing a company's financial stability see page 73.)

Certificates of Deposit

Certificates of deposit (CDs) can be an excellent investment for a college-bound child over age 14, especially since the money will be needed in five years or less. With a CD you deposit a stated amount of money—often $500, $1,000, or more—and you're guaranteed a stated interest rate at the end of a stated period. When purchasing CDs, you should comparison-shop for the highest interest rates and make sure that all deposits are insured by the FDIC. Also ask about any penalties for early withdrawal: you never know if you'll need the money before freshman year.

The College Savings Bank of Princeton, New Jersey, offers a special CD designed just for college saving. The variable interest rate adjusts each year with the College Board's Independent College 500 Index, a measure of the yearly rise in college tuition, fees, and room and board. The idea is simple: You pay a set price for the CD today, and you'll be guaranteed that it will cover your child's college costs when the time comes.

The CollegeSure CDs don't pay an interest rate equal to the actual index rate: they return 1 percentage point less on denominations of $10,000 or more, 1.5 points less on smaller amounts. They make up the difference by starting with an initial investment about 10 percent higher than current college costs.

For example, if you were to deposit $2,100 in a CollegeSure account in 1993, it would be worth about $5,100 in the year 2008 if college costs increase by an average of 7.5 percent annually, or $7,200 if college costs increase by 10 percent annually. (The program guarantees a minimum annual percentage rate return of 4 percent a year.)

If you faithfully contributed to the CollegeSure account and your child ultimately decided not to attend college, you could get your money back, plus interest. For additional information on the program, contact the College Savings Bank, 5 Vaughn Drive, Princeton, NJ 08540-6313; (800) 888-2723.

Mutual Funds

When you put your money in a mutual fund, your cash goes into a common pool along with the deposits of other investors. The company then invests the money on behalf of all the contributors. Each investor is really a shareholder who owns a proportionate share of the fund's assets. By investing in a mutual fund, you can invest $1,000 and enjoy some of the same rates of return as someone who invests $20,000. You can also reduce your risk because the mutual fund's assets will be spread out among many different investments.

With more than 3,700 mutual funds to choose from, selecting a fund can be difficult. You should first narrow your search by looking for a fund that carries a level of risk that you're comfortable with. Again, you face the same risk-benefit trade-off: mutual funds that offer the highest returns carry the greatest risks, and vice versa. (For a summary of some of the different types of mutual funds, see the box below.)

401(k) and Other Retirement Accounts

For some parents one of the best ways to be ready to pay for college is to fully fund their retirement account, then borrow money from it to pay the tuition bills. Under current tax laws you can borrow from a tax-deferred 401(k) savings plan in order to pay for college. Of course, you can't be sure that the same rules will be in place when it's time for your child to begin college.

If your employer offers a 401(k) retirement account, consider

---

TYPES OF MUTUAL FUNDS

• **Aggressive growth funds** attempt to maximize capital gains; some may invest in speculative stocks that are expected to grow.

• **Balanced funds** attempt to balance three investment goals: conserving principal, paying dividends or current income, and promoting long-term growth. Balanced funds tend to be relatively conservative: investments include a mix of bonds with preferred and common stock.

• **Bond funds** invest in corporate and government bonds; they produce a steady income. The risk of the fund depends on the holdings: some funds buy only highly rated bonds; others choose higher-yield but riskier issues.

• **Ginnie Mae funds** invest in mortgage securities backed by the Government National Mortgage Association.

• **Global equity funds** invest in securities that are traded worldwide.

• **Growth funds** strive for long-term capital appreciation, but they invest heavily in blue chip stocks with a record of steady growth rather than highly speculative stocks.

• **Money market funds** invest in short-term securities sold in the money market. These are generally the safest, most stable securities available, including Treasury bills and CDs of large banks.

• **Tax-exempt funds** invest in government and other tax-free bonds.

investing in it whether or not you intend to borrow against the money for college. These retirement accounts allow you to contribute a set amount of before-tax dollars (between 6 and 10 percent of your salary); in some cases employers make matching contributions as well. You delay paying tax on this money until you retire and presumably fall to a lower income-tax bracket.

As with other retirement plans, there's a penalty for withdrawing the money before age 59fi. But unlike other retirement accounts, 401(k) plans contain "hardship" and loan provisions that make money available for certain emergencies—including paying college tuition.

Another benefit: The money kept in a retirement account doesn't show up on a financial aid form under the current rules. This could possibly increase your child's chances of qualifying for grants and low-interest loans, if you will be applying for financial aid. However, you can't be sure what the rules will be by the time your child is ready for college.

Before taking out a loan to pay for school, you should be sure you can pay it back. You are borrowing from your retirement nest egg, and you probably can't afford to use the money without replacing it. Currently such loans must be paid back within five years to protect the integrity of the retirement account. If you borrow a lot of money, it could be a real hardship to repay in just a few years. And loans not repaid within five years are subject to a 10 percent penalty.

If your employer offers a 401(k) retirement plan, expect to use it to fund your retirement. As an added benefit you might be able to enjoy the possibility of borrowing against it to fund your child's education or to make up the difference between the money you have been able to save and the final tuition bill.

403(b) plans are retirement accounts for employees of educational institutions or nonprofit organizations; they are basically the nonprofit sector's answer to 401(k) plans. Participants can typically withdraw up to $50,000 without incurring penalties if it is paid back within five years.

Self-employed people can set up a Keogh plan to finance their retirement. Owner-employees (those who own more than 10 percent of the business) may borrow up to half the amount in the account, up to $50,000. The same penalties apply to the terms of these loans as to 401(k) loans.

Annuities and Life Insurance

Annuities are contracts sold by life insurance companies in which you pay a certain amount of money, and the company agrees to a certain payout schedule, often either a lump sum or regular monthly payments. Most annuities are used for retirement financing, but they can be used for college funding as well. Like bonds, annuities promise a guaranteed income, but they can be quite complicated when it comes to the payouts and tax consequences. With annuities interest accumulates without being subject to tax until the money is withdrawn.

In general, annuities aren't wise investments for college because of the tax consequences. Yes, the value of the annuity will grow to a tidy sum in 10 or 15 years, but the money isn't all yours: you'll have to share with Uncle Sam. For example, if you bought a $10,000 annuity that was worth $40,000 in 15 years, you'd owe about $8,500 in taxes if you were in the 28 percent tax bracket. You're not through paying: unless you will be 59fi years old or older when it's time to send your child to college, you'll have to pay an additional 10 percent excise tax on the money you take out. For most parents the tax liability and penalties offset the gains and make annuities less appealing for college saving than other investment options.

Cash-value life insurance policies for children face many of the same obstacles. (For more information on life insurance see Chapter 4.)

Home-Equity Loans

If you own a house, you may be able to borrow against the equity in your home to pay for college. As long as the money is used to pay for educational expenses, the interest on the loan remains tax deductible. The amount of the loan you would qualify for is based on the market value of your house minus the amount you still owe on it. For example, if your house is worth $100,000 and you owe $30,000 on your mortgage, you have $70,000 in equity in your house. You can probably get a loan of up to 80 percent of $70,000, or $56,000.

A second mortgage is a form of equity loan that provides you with a specified amount of money at a fixed rate of interest, and it provides for repayment following a set schedule of monthly installments. You'll have to pay points and closing costs, but the rate is usually cheaper than that on a personal loan. The other type of home-equity loan works more like a credit card: You are given a credit limit and you can draw on the money at any time. The costs of borrowing the money are often quite high, and this revolving line of credit can promote irresponsible spending.

Home-equity loans involve significant risks, including the possibility of losing your home if you're unable to pay the debt. If you plan to apply for a home-equity loan, anticipate additional closing fees, attorneys' fees, appraisal fees, and points. And allow plenty of time for the process: it can take months to complete all the paperwork.

ISSUES TO DISCUSS:
WHAT PARENTS SHOULD TALK ABOUT

- Do we want to save money to pay for our child's college education or do we want to depend on scholarships and financial aid (if it is available)?
- Do we want to send our child to private or parochial primary and secondary schools? If so, how will this affect our college savings plans?
- Do we want our child to contribute to the college fund by working part time and during the summer?
- How much debt are we willing to assume to educate our child?
- What are our long-term savings goals?
- How much will we have to save to reach those goals?
- Who will be responsible for managing the college funds?
- Should we put the funds in an account in the child's name?
- Where should we go for investment advice?

QUESTIONS & ANSWERS

I have heard of prepaid tuition programs. Should I pay now or pay later?

The best strategy is probably to pay later, but save now. Prepaid tuition plans typically allow you to pay tuition at today's rate and enroll your child in the school when the time comes. In many cases you can pay for freshman year when your babe is still in diapers.

DOLLARS FOR SCHOLARS: FINANCIAL AID

All too often middle-class parents simply assume that their children won't be eligible for financial aid and never check into the possibilities. They may be shortchanging themselves. Everyone should apply for aid.

Though the financial aid options available when your child reaches college age will certainly be different, this is a brief summary of federal financial aid programs available today. This may give you a broad idea of financing options:

• **Pell Grants**. Grants of $200 to $2100 per year, based on financial need, not academic achievement. The average grant: $1,290. Pell grants are entitlements: if a student qualifies, he or she automatically receives the money. The student must apply for this grant before he or she can be considered for other federal aid. The student applies for the grant by filling out the federal government's Application for Student Financial Aid.

• **Supplemental Educational Opportunity Grants**. Grants of from $200 to $4,000 per year, based on need. SEOG is a federal program that supplements Pell grants. Under this program funds are awarded directly to colleges, which in turn dispense the money. These grants are awarded at the discretion of the college or university; they are intended for families with the lowest incomes. To apply, a student should request information directly from the financial aid offices of the college he or she will attend.

• **Perkins Loan**. Low-interest loans to students based on need. The amount available varies with the program: up to $4,500 for students in vocational programs who have completed less than two years of study toward a bachelor's degree, $9,000 for undergraduates who already have completed two years of study, and $18,000 for graduate and professional students. The amount of aid any individual student receives depends on financial need, other aid received, and the availability of funds. It's entirely up to the school to decide how to divide the money; a Perkins loan is not an entitlement.

• **Stafford Loans (formerly known as Guaranteed Student Loans)**. Federally insured and subsidized loans offered through private lenders. Loans of $2,625 available to undergraduates, $4,000 to upperclassmen, and $7,500 to graduate students each year.

• **College Work-Study Program**. Minimum-wage or near-minimum-wage jobs for needy students; the programs are administered by each college or university.

The details of each program vary from year to year. For information on how to apply for financial aid, refer to "The Student Guide," a reference manual for federal government financial assistance, which is issued each year by the Department of Education. For a free copy contact the Federal Student Aid Information Center, P.O. Box 84, Washington, DC 20044; (800) 433-3243.

In addition to government programs, many credit unions, fraternal organizations, employers, military organizations, and local groups provide private scholarships. Start by asking groups you're affiliated with whether they offer any scholarships based on either need, academic qualifications, community service, or some other criteria.

Sounds good, but there are a few problems. Your total costs wouldn't be covered: you'd still need to come up with the money for room, board, and junk food. And what if your child doesn't want to go to college? Or doesn't want to go to the school that you've paid for? Do you want your musical prodigy to forfeit a chance to study at Juilliard just because you've already paid for tuition at Michigan State?

In most cases if your child doesn't enroll in the school, you get back the money you paid—but you forfeit the interest. Ouch. Most parents find it makes more sense to allow their children to choose a college based on their educational needs and interests rather than on a financial decision made 15 or 18 years earlier.

Can I use my series EE bonds to pay for any educational expense?

No, eligible educational expenses include tuition and fees (such as lab fees and other course expenses) at colleges, universities, technical institutes, and vocational schools. Room and board, book fees, and costs associated with sports, games, or hobbies aren't eligible.

I have children who are ready to enter college. We applied for financial aid and were told we could afford to pay $15,000 a year. I don't have that kind of money. Where did the financial aid officers get the idea that I did?

When estimating the family contribution to college costs, financial aid services look at income, assets, and liabilities. The amount you are expected to contribute includes your potential to borrow and secure other types of loans, not just your ability to pay out of your current income or bank balance. You might not have an extra $15,000 in a savings account, but you might be able to borrow that amount, perhaps by taking out a home-equity loan.

Our family's income is too high to qualify for the tax deduction for series EE bonds. Can I still get any tax benefits?

Perhaps. If you make too much money to qualify for the federal tax exemption, you may still be able to benefit from buying series EE bonds by purchasing the bonds in your child's name. If you do this, you may be able to reduce the amount of tax you owe. If the bonds mature when your child is 14 years old or older, the taxable interest income is taxed at your child's rate.

Are scholarship-finding services worth the fees?

Not usually. Most of these services promise to provide you with a list of potential scholarships matched to your child's specific skills and interests. For the $50 to $100 fee you probably won't learn anything you wouldn't learn from talking to your child's high school guidance counselor or by reviewing books on financial aid in your local library. Many programs tell you that millions of dollars in private scholarship aid goes unawarded every year because people don't apply for it, but what they don't say is that many of these programs are designed by employers for children of their employees. Spend an evening in the library and save the money for tuition.

My daughter was given several EE bonds, which I seem to have misplaced during a recent move. What should I do?

All you have to do is contact the Bureau of the Public Debt and the bond will be replaced without cost. If possible, enclose a record of the bonds: their issue dates and serial numbers. Contact: Bureau of the Public Debt, Savings Bond Operations, Parkersburg, WV 26106-1328. You can speed the process along by filling out Form FD 1048 in the case of a lost or stolen bond or Form FD 1934 in the case of a mutilated or partially destroyed bond. The forms are usually available from local banks or federal reserve banks. The reissued bonds will bear the original issue date.

My daughter received a $500 scholarship from the local Lions club. When her school's financial aid officer heard about it, he reduced her financial aid. What good does it do to apply for scholarships if it doesn't decrease the amount we pay?

Scholarships can decrease your final bill, depending on how the school credits the scholarship money. For example, if the $500 goes toward reducing the amount of your child's loan (which you have to pay back) rather than the amount of a grant (which you don't pay back), then you're $500 ahead of the game. Talk the issue over with the financial aid officer; it can't hurt to ask for a break.

STEP BY STEP: COLLEGE SAVINGS CHECKLIST

- ❏ Establish a savings goal based on the projected costs of college.
- ❏ Estimate how much you will have to save each month to reach your goal. You may aim for half the cost of tuition or less, planning to borrow or turn to financial-aid programs for assistance when the time comes.
- ❏ Consider various investment options.
- ❏ Collect references of a number of financial planners if you feel you need assistance in planning a college savings program.
- ❏ Work out a long-term savings plan.
- ❏ Save, save, save. Make college fund deposits a budgeted part of your monthly expenditures, just like a mortgage payment.
- ❏ Review your investment and savings plan every few years—or when the tax laws change or your child approaches age 14—to make sure your strategy remains the best option for your child.

HOW MUCH DO YOU NEED TO SAVE?

Once you've committed yourself to regular savings, you need to figure out what your monthly savings goals should be. The following tables can serve as a guide; the calculations are based on investments earning 7 percent interest, compounded monthly.

To save $25,000 . . .

in 1 year you need to save	$	2,017 a month
in 5 years you need to save	$	349 a month
in 10 years you need to save	$	144 a month
in 15 years you need to save	$	79 a month
in 16 years you need to save	$	71 a month
in 17 years you need to save	$	64 a month
in 18 years you need to save	$	58 a month

To save $50,000 . . .

in 1 year you need to save	$	4,035 a month
in 5 years you need to save	$	698 a month
in 10 years you need to save	$	289 a month
in 15 years you need to save	$	158 a month
in 16 years you need to save	$	142 a month
in 17 years you need to save	$	128 a month
in 18 years you need to save	$	116 a month

To save $75,000 . . .

in 1 year you need to save	$	6,052 a month
in 5 years you need to save	$	1,048 a month
in 10 years you need to save	$	433 a month
in 15 years you need to save	$	237 a month
in 16 years you need to save	$	213 a month
in 17 years you need to save	$	192 a month
in 18 years you need to save	$	174 a month

To save $100,000 . . .

in 1 year you need to save	$	8,069 a month
in 5 years you need to save	$	1,397 a month
in 10 years you need to save	$	578 a month
in 15 years you need to save	$	315 a month
in 16 years you need to save	$	284 a month
in 17 years you need to save	$	256 a month
in 18 years you need to save	$	232 a month

To save $150,000...

in 1 year you need to save	$ 12,104 a month
in 5 years you need to save	$ 2,095 a month
in 10 years you need to save	$ 867 a month
in 15 years you need to save	$ 473 a month
in 16 years you need to save	$ 426 a month
in 17 years you need to save	$ 384 a month
in 18 years you need to save	$ 348 a month

To save $200,000...

in 1 year you need to save	$ 16,139 a month
in 5 years you need to save	$ 2,794 a month
in 10 years you need to save	$ 1,156 a month
in 15 years you need to save	$ 631 a month
in 16 years you need to save	$ 568 a month
in 17 years you need to save	$ 513 a month
in 18 years you need to save	$ 464 a month

To save $250,000...

in 1 year you need to save	$ 20,173 a month
in 5 years you need to save	$ 3,492 a month
in 10 years you need to save	$ 1,444 a month
in 15 years you need to save	$ 789 a month
in 16 years you need to save	$ 710 a month
in 17 years you need to save	$ 641 a month
in 18 years you need to save	$ 580 a month

To save $300,000...

in 1 year you need to save	$ 24,208 a month
in 5 years you need to save	$ 4,190 a month
in 10 years you need to save	$ 1,733 a month
in 15 years you need to save	$ 946 a month
in 16 years you need to save	$ 852 a month
in 17 years you need to save	$ 769 a month
in 18 years you need to save	$ 697 a month

To save $350,000...

in 1 year you need to save	$ 28,243 a month
in 5 years you need to save	$ 4,889 a month
in 10 years you need to save	$ 2,022 a month
in 15 years you need to save	$ 1,104 a month
in 16 years you need to save	$ 994 a month
in 17 years you need to save	$ 897 a month
in 18 years you need to save	$ 813 a month

RESOURCES:
WHERE TO GO FOR MORE INFORMATION

BOOKS

■ **Financing a College Education: The Essential Guide for the 90s**, by Judith B. Margolin. Cost: $14.95, plus about $3 shipping and handling. Contact: Plenum Press, Attention: Order Department, 233 Spring Street, New York, NY 10013; (800) 221-9369.

■ **How to Pay for a College Education Without Going Broke**, by Richard W. Lewis. Cost: $9.95, plus $3.75 shipping and handling. Contact: Bob Adams, Inc., Publishers, 260 Center Street, Holbrook, Massachusetts, 02343; (800) 872-5627.

BROCHURES

■ "Catalog of Services and Publications in Standard & Poor's," by Standard & Poor's. Cost: Free. Contact: Public Relations Department, Standard & Poor's, 25 Broadway, New York, NY 10004; (800) 221-5277, (212) 208-8000.

■ "The College Money Guide," Octameron Associates. Cost: Free. Contact: Octameron Associates, Inc., Box 2748, Alexandria, VA 22301; (703) 836-5480.

■ "The Consumer Guide to Comprehensive Financial Planning," by the International Association for Financial Planning. Cost: Free. Contact: International Association for Financial Planning, Two Concourse Parkway, Suite 800, Atlanta, GA 30328; (404) 395-1605, (800) 945-4237.

■ "Facts About Financial Planners," by the U.S. Federal Trade Commission. Cost: 50 cents. Contact: Consumer Information Center—3B, P.O. Box 100, Pueblo, CO 81002.

■ "Financial Strategies for New Parents," by the International Association for Financial Planning. Cost: Free. Contact: International Association for Financial Planning, Two Concourse Parkway, Suite 800, Atlanta, GA 30328; (404) 395-1605, (800) 945-4237.

■ "Investment Income and Expenses," (Publication 550) by the Internal Revenue Service. Cost: Free. Call: (800) 829-3676.

■ "Investor's Information Kit," by New York Stock Exchange. (Contains a number of booklets, including Glossary, Understanding Stocks and Bonds, Understanding Financial Statements, Getting Help When You Invest, and the Margin Trading Guide.) Cost: $12.00. Contact: New York Stock Exchange Publications, P.O. Box 5020, Farmingdale, NY 11736; (516) 454-1800, extension 356.

■ "Preparing Your Child for College: A Resource Book for Parents," by the U.S. Department of Education. Cost: Free. Contact: Consumer Information Center—3C, P.O. Box 100, Pueblo, CO 81002.

■ "Selecting a Qualified Financial Planning Professional: Twelve Questions to Consider," by the Institute of Certified Financial Planners. Cost: Free. Contact: Institute of Certified Financial Planners, 7600 East Eastman Avenue, Suite 301, Denver, CO 80231-4397; (800) 282-7526, (303) 751-7600.

■ "The Student Guide," by the U.S. Department of Education. Cost: Free. Contact: Federal Student Aid Information Center, P.O. Box 84, Washington, DC 20044; (800) 433-3243.

■ "Your Children's College Bill: How to Figure It . . . How to Pay for It," by the Institute of Certified Financial Planners. Cost: Free. Contact: Institute of Certified Financial Planners, 7600 East Eastman Avenue, Suite 301, Denver, CO 80231-4397; (800) 282-7526, (303) 751-7600.

■ Mutual Funds. Information on mutual funds is available from the Investment Company Institute. Titles include:

• **"Planning for College? The Mutual Fund Advantage"**
• **"What Is a Mutual Fund?"**
• **"An Investor's Guide to Reading the Mutual Fund Prospectus"**
• **"Money-Market Mutual Funds: A Part of Every Financial Plan"**
• **"Mutual Fund Fact Book"**

Cost: Free. Contact: Investment Company Institute, 1600 M Street NW, Washington, DC 20036; (202) 955-3534.

■ U.S. Savings Bonds. Information on U.S. Savings Bonds, by the Department of Treasury. Cost: Free. Contact: Office of Public Affairs, U.S. Savings Bond Division, Washington, DC 20226. Available titles:

- "U.S. Savings Bonds Buyer's Guide"
- "The Savings Bonds Question and Answer Book"
- "Table of Interest Accrual Dates"
- "Table of Redemption Values"
- "Current Market-Based Rate Announcement"

For market rates call (800) 4US-BONDS. Write for free brochures.

GLOSSARY: UNDERSTANDING THE TERMS

Controlled inflation: A period when the rate of inflation remains steady.

No-load mutual fund: A mutual fund that sells its shares without charging a commission. The load is the sales charge or commission assessed by mutual funds to cover their selling costs.

Risk: The relative likelihood that the money being invested will be lost. Investments with greater risk offer greater rewards; high-interest investments tend to be high-risk investments.

Triple-tax exempt: An investment that is exempt from federal, state, and local income taxes.

CHAPTER 10

SETTING YOUR RECORDS STRAIGHT

NUTS AND BOLTS

Sifting through mounds of papers can be time consuming and tedious when you first get organized, but in the long run good record keeping will save you time and aggravation. Registering your child for kindergarten won't seem like such a daunting task when you can put your finger on a copy of your child's birth certificate and immunization charts. And updating your life insurance and rewriting your last will and testament will be a snap when your policies and financial data are organized and easy to find.

You will probably find it easiest to store your important papers in four locations:

- Your attorney's office;
- A safe-deposit box;
- An at-home active file;
- An at-home storage box.

What belongs where? The checklist and work sheets in this chapter will help you create a practical filing system. While some of the information on the work sheets may seem obvious, filling out the forms will save you time by giving you a quick reference list—and it may someday save your heirs a lot of headaches and hassles. Once your papers are in order, you will find it easier to keep an eye on your legal and financial matters. Now is the time to get organized: Ready, aim, file.

FOLLOWING THE PAPER TRAIL

If you've hunted through your file marked important papers and you still can't find a copy of your birth certificate, marriage certificate, or divorce decree (even though you know it's there somewhere), consider giving up and obtaining certified duplicate copies from your state office of vital records. Some states charge a nominal fee—usually $5 or so—per copy. When writing for certificates of birth, death, marriage, or divorce, be sure to include the following information:

BIRTH OR DEATH RECORD

- Full legal name of the person on the record;
- Sex of the person;
- The person's parents' names, including mother's maiden name;
- Month, day, and year of birth or death;
- City, county, and state where birth or death occurred;
- The name of the hospital where the event took place, if known;
- Your relationship to the person whose record you are requesting (many states will provide records only to the person named on the certificate, immediate family members, or legal representatives of the person);
- The reason you need the copy;
- Payment (most states charge between $5 and $15 for a certified copy—many states accept credit cards);
- Your return address, phone number, and signature.

MARRIAGE RECORDS

- Full legal names of the bride and groom;
- Month, day, and year of marriage;

- City, county, and state where marriage took place;
- The reason you need a copy;
- Your relationship to the person whose record you are requesting.

DIVORCE RECORDS

- Full legal names of the husband and wife;
- Month, day, and year of divorce or annulment;
- City, county, and state of divorce or annulment;
- Type of decree: divorce or annulment?
- The reason you need a copy;
- Your relationship to the person whose record you are requesting.

In some states older records must be obtained from county clerks' offices or state archives. For a list of state offices of vital records see the Resources section.

ISSUES TO DISCUSS: WHAT PARENTS SHOULD TALK ABOUT

- ❏ Who should be responsible for maintaining our family files?
- ❏ To whom should we tell the location of our records?
- ❏ Where should we get a safe-deposit box?
- ❏ Where should we keep the key to the safe-deposit box?
- ❏ Where should we keep our at-home records?
- ❏ Where should we store our inactive files?

QUESTIONS & ANSWERS

Should we keep our wills and life insurance policies in our safe-deposit box?

Never. In most states when the owner or joint owner of a safe-deposit box dies, the bank must seal the box until the estate is settled. In order to obtain a copy of the will and life insurance policy, your heirs would have to get legal permission to open the box. That can slow down progress on settling your estate since the life insurance company won't pay the claim until the policy is surrendered, and the original will is required to probate the estate. Instead keep your life insurance policies in a file at home and the original of your will with your attorney (with a copy in the safe-deposit box).

I've searched everywhere and can't find my birth certificate. What now?

Give up and get another one. You can obtain a duplicate copy by contacting the department of vital records in the state you were born. For details, see "Following the Paper Trail" on page 202.

In the back of a dusty drawer I found a statement from a savings account I opened in another state 15 years ago. I haven't received a statement or heard from the bank since I moved out of the state. Is the money still mine?

It'll be yours to spend just as soon as you stake your claim with your state's bureau of unclaimed property. Abandoned bank accounts, forgotten security deposits to landlords and utility companies, uncollected insurance proceeds, and unclaimed inheritances from deceased relatives total more than $3 billion in unclaimed funds each year. After the bank or financial institute makes a good-faith effort to locate the owner, the money held in dormant accounts passes to the state. But this is not a case of finders keepers: you are entitled to the money, though the state government usually gets to keep any interest the money has earned. To claim your forgotten funds, call your state bureau of unclaimed funds.

How long do I need to keep my tax records?

If you are unfortunate enough to be audited by the Internal Revenue Service, you had better have three years of records on hand, including the scraps of paper and receipts for your deductions. The IRS auditor won't be concerned with your older records, but you might want to keep copies of your final income-tax returns as part of your financial history.

How do I go about getting a safe-deposit box?

You can rent a safe-deposit box from a local bank for about $20 to $30 a year, depending on the size of the box. It's up to you to decide who should have a key to the box, but in most cases you should authorize someone else to open the box just in case you can't do it yourself. An inventory of the contents of your safe-deposit box should be kept in your home file, as well as copies of important documents stored in the box. A word of caution: Most banks don't insure the contents of safe-deposit boxes against theft or damage. Ask your homeowner's insurance agent about the cost of an insurance floater for valuables such as jewelry stored in a safe-deposit box.

My husband and I are planning a vacation overseas. Does our nine-month-old daughter need a passport?

You bet. The rules for applying for a passport are somewhat different for a minor. Passports for children under age 18 are good for only 5 years; passports for adults are good for 10 years. For information on obtaining a passport for your child call the U.S. State Department's Office of Passport Services at (202) 647-0518.

STEP BY STEP: GETTING-ORGANIZED CHECKLIST

WHAT TO STORE WITH YOUR LAWYER

- ❑ Last will (the original)
- ❑ Living will
- ❑ Power of attorney
- ❑ Advance medical directive (or durable medical power of attorney)
- ❑ Safe-deposit key (duplicate)
- ❑ Letters of instruction (including information on burial instructions and any prepaid funeral plans or plots)

WHAT TO PUT IN YOUR SAFE-DEPOSIT BOX

Personal Papers

- ❑ Birth certificates
- ❑ Death certificates
- ❑ Marriage certificates
- ❑ Divorce decree

- ❑ Citizenship papers
- ❑ Last will (copy)
- ❑ Passports
- ❑ Military service records
- ❑ Veterans Administration papers
- ❑ Adoption papers
- ❑ Social Security verification
- ❑ Letters of instruction (copy)
- ❑ Power of attorney (copy)

Financial Papers

- ❑ Stock certificates
- ❑ Bonds
- ❑ Mutual fund certificates
- ❑ Automobile titles
- ❑ Real estate deeds
- ❑ Contracts/IOUs
- ❑ Household inventory (including photographs)
- ❑ Home records (surveys, blueprints, improvements)
- ❑ Insurance policies (copies)
- ❑ Retirement and pension plan documents

WHAT TO PUT IN YOUR AT-HOME FILES

Personal

- ❑ WORK SHEET: Location of Important Papers
- ❑ WORK SHEET: Personal Information
- ❑ WORK SHEET: Records at a Glance
- ❑ WORK SHEET: Your Child's Immunization Record
- ❑ Employment records
- ❑ Education history
- ❑ Professional accomplishments
- ❑ Memberships in professional and fraternal organizations
- ❑ Medical records
- ❑ Birth certificates (copy)
- ❑ Death certificates (copy)
- ❑ Family medical records
- ❑ Cemetery records

FINANCIAL

- ❏ Unpaid bills
- ❏ Bank statements
- ❏ Broker's statements
- ❏ Canceled checks (6 years)
- ❏ Credit-card information
- ❏ Insurance policies (originals)
  Auto
  Disability
  Homeowner's
  Life
  Medical
  Other
- ❏ Mortgage information
- ❏ Other loan information
- ❏ Appliance manuals and warranties (including list of date and place of purchase and receipts)
- ❏ Home-improvement records (until house is sold and taxes are paid)
- ❏ Tax receipts and working papers
- ❏ Tax returns (6 years)
- ❏ Broker's transaction advances

What to Keep in Storage

- ❏ Tax returns (more than 6 years old)
- ❏ Family health records (more than 3 years old)
- ❏ Canceled checks (important debts only after 6 years)
- ❏ Proof that major debts have been paid off
- ❏ Home-improvement records (after house is sold)

PERSONAL INFORMATION

	You	Your Spouse
Full legal name		
Address		
City, state, zip		
Telephone number		
Employer		
Telephone number at work		
Date of birth		
Place of birth		
Social Security number		

	Child 1	Child 2
Full legal name		
Address		
City, state, zip		
Telephone number		
Employer		
Telephone number at work		
Date of birth		
Place of birth		
Social Security number		
Name of spouse, if any		

	Child 3	Child 4
Full legal name		
Address		
City, state, zip		
Telephone number		
Employer		
Telephone number at work		
Date of birth		
Place of birth		
Social Security number		
Name of spouse, if any		

	Parents	Spouse's Parents
Full legal name		
Address		
City, state, zip		
Telephone number		
Date of birth		
Place of birth		
Social Security number		
Mother's maiden name		

PERSONAL CONTACTS

Relationship	Name	Address	Phone	Fax
Accountant				
Attorney				
Banker				
Clergyman				
Executor of estate				
Friend				

Insurance agents:

Auto				
Disability				
Homeowner's				
Life				
Medical				
Other				
Neighbor				
Next of kin				
Physician				
Work contact				

LOCATION OF IMPORTANT PAPERS

Document	Location of Original	Location of Copy
Personal Papers		
Birth certificates		
Death certificates		
Marriage certificates		
Divorce decrees		
Wills		
Living wills		
Military records		
Citizenship papers		
Passports		
Social Security cards		
Adoption papers		
Educational records		
Financial Papers		
Insurance policies		
Disability		
Homeowner's		
Life		
Medical		
Other		
Mortgage papers		
Deeds to real estate		
Automobile titles		
Inventory of safe-deposit box		

RECORDS AT A GLANCE

CASH ACCOUNTS

Type of Account	Name of Institution	Account Number	Interest Rate	Location of Records
Checking accounts				
Savings accounts				
Credit union accounts				
Other cash				

INVESTMENTS

Type of Account	Name of Institution	Account Number	Amount Invested	Maturity Date	Interest Rate	Location of Records
Money market fund						
Certificates of deposit						
Treasury bills						
Other						

STOCKS AND MUTUAL FUNDS

Name of Company	Number of Shares	Date Purchased	Cost	Annual Income	Location of Certificate
1.					
2.					
3.					
4.					
5.					

BONDS (CORPORATE AND MUNICIPAL)

Name of Company	Face Amount	Date of Purchase	Maturity Date	Interest Rate	Annual Income	Location of Records
1.						
2.						
3.						
4.						
5.						

REAL ESTATE

Location:

Date purchased:

Cost:

Current market value/date:

Improvements:

Location of records:

RETIREMENT ACCOUNTS

Type of Account	Name of Participant	Name of Company	Present Value	Location of Records
Annuities				
Pensions				
Profit-sharing plan				
Individual retirement acct.				
401(k) plans				
Keogh plans				

INSURANCE

Type of Insurance	Name of Company	Policy Number	Location of Policy
Auto			
Disability			
Homeowner's			
Health			
Life			
Umbrella			
Other			

Life Insurance

Insured: _____

Company: _____

Type of policy: _____

Policy number: _____

Face amount: _____

Beneficiary: _____

Cash value: _____

Amount borrowed: _____

Location of policy: _____

CREDIT CARDS

Type of Card	Issuing Institution	Account Number	Authorized Users	Balance Due	Location of Records
1.					
2.					
3.					
4.					
5.					
6.					
7.					
8.					
9.					
10.					

DEBTS

Type of Loan	Lender	Amount of Loan	Interest Rate	Balance Due	Monthly Payment	Location of Records
Car loan						
Education loan						
Home improvement						
Other						

Mortgage

Mortgage holder:

Mortgage balance:

Interest rate:

Monthly payments:

YOUR CHILD'S IMMUNIZATION RECORD

Name:

Birth date:

Type of Shot	Dose	Recommended At	Date Given
OPV (oral polio vaccine)	1st	2 months	
	2nd	4 months	
	3rd	15 months	
	4th	Before school	
DPT (diphtheria-pertussis-tetanus)	1st	2 months	
	2nd	4 months	
	3rd	6 months	
	4th	15 months	
	5th	Before starting school (4–6 years)	
	Adult booster	Every 10 years (diphtheria and tetanus)	
MMR (measles-mumps-rubella)	1st	15 months	
	2nd	Before starting school (4–6 years)	
Hib (bacterial meningitis)	1st	2 months	
	2nd	4 months	
	3rd	6 months	
	4th	15 months	
HBV (hepatitis B virus)	1st	At birth	
	2nd	1–2 months	
	3rd	6–18 months	

RESOURCES:
WHERE TO GO FOR MORE INFORMATION

BROCHURES AND SOFTWARE

■ "Where to Write for Vital Records," by the U.S. Department of Health and Human Services. Cost: $1.75 (send check or money order made out to Superintendent of Documents). Contact: Consumer Information Center, P.O. Box 100, Pueblo, CO 81002.

■ "Nolo's Personal RecordKeeper," by Carol Pladsen and Attorney Ralph Warner. Software for IBM or Macintosh computers. Includes a 320-page manual. Cost: $49.95, plus $4 shipping and handling. Contact: Nolo Press, 950 Parker Street, Berkeley, CA 94710; (800) 992-6656.

STATE OFFICES OF VITAL RECORDS

ALABAMA
Vital Records
P.O. Box 5625
Montgomery, AL 36103
(205)613-5481

ALASKA
Department of Health and Social
    Services
Bureau of Vital Statistics
P.O. Box 110675
Juneau, AK 99811-0675
(907) 465-3391

ARIZONA
Vital Records Section
Arizona Department of Health
    Services
P.O. Box 3887
Phoenix, AZ 85030
(602) 255-3260

ARKANSAS
Division of Vital Records
Arkansas Department of Health
4815 West Markham Street, Slot 44
Little Rock, AR 72205
(501) 661-2336

CALIFORNIA
Vital Statistics Section
Office of State Registrar
304 S Street
P.O. Box 730241
Sacramento, CA 94244-0241
(916) 445-2684

COLORADO
Vital Records Section
Colorado Department of Health
4300 Cherry Creek Drive South
Denver, CO 80222-1530
(303) 756-4464

CONNECTICUT
Vital Records Unit
State Department of Health Services
150 Washington Street
Hartford, CT 06106
(203) 566-1124

DELAWARE
Office of Vital Statistics
Division of Public Health
P.O. Box 637
Dover, DE 19903
(302) 739-4721

DISTRICT OF COLUMBIA
Vital Records Branch
613 G Street NW, 9th Floor
Washington, DC 20001
(202) 727-5316

FLORIDA
Department of Health and
   Rehabilitative Services
Office of Vital Statistics
P.O. Box 210
Jacksonville, FL 32231
(904) 359-6900

GEORGIA
Georgia Department of Human
   Resources
Vital Records Unit
Room 217-H
47 Trinity Avenue SW
Atlanta, GA 30334
(404) 656-4900

HAWAII
Vital Records Section
State Department of Health
P.O. Box 3378
Honolulu, HI 96801
(808) 586-4533

IDAHO
Bureau of Vital Statistics
State Department of Health
   and Welfare
Statehouse
P.O. Box 83720
Boise, ID 83720-0036
(208) 334-5988

ILLINOIS
Division of Vital Records
State Department of Health
605 West Jefferson Street
Springfield, IL 62702-5097
(217) 782-6553

INDIANA
Division of Vital Records
State Board of Health
1330 West Michigan Street,
   Room 111
P.O. Box 1964
Indianapolis, IN 46206-1964
(317) 633-0274

IOWA
Iowa Department of Public Health
Vital Records Section
Lucas Office Building
321 E. 12th Street, 4th Floor
Des Moines, IA 50319-0075
(515) 281-5871

KANSAS
Office of Vital Statistics
Kansas State Department of Health
   and Environment
900 Southwest Jackson Street
Topeka, KS 66612-2221
(913) 296-1400

KENTUCKY
Office of Vital Statistics
Department of Health Services
275 East Main Street
Frankfort, KY 40621
(502) 564-4212

LOUISIANA
Vital Records Registry
P.O. Box 60630
New Orleans, LA 70160
(504) 568-5152

MAINE
Office of Vital Records
Human Services Building
221 State Street
Augusta, ME 04333-0011
(207) 287-3181

MARYLAND
Division of Vital Records
P.O. Box 68760
Baltimore, MD 21215
(410) 225-5988

MASSACHUSETTS
Registry of Vital Records
   and Statistics
Department of Public Health
150 Tremont Street, Room B-3
Boston, MA 02111
(617) 727-0110

MICHIGAN
Office of the State Registrar and
   Center for Health Statistics
Michigan Department of
   Public Health
P.O. Box 30195
Lansing, MI 48909
(517) 335-8655

MINNESOTA
Minnesota Department of Health
Section of Vital Records
717 Delaware Street, SE
Minneapolis, MN 55414
(612) 623-5121

MISSISSIPPI
Vital Records
State Board of Health
P.O. Box 1700
Jackson, MS 39215
(601) 960-7981

MISSOURI
Department of Health
Bureau of Vital Records
P.O. Box 570
Jefferson City, MO 65102
(314) 751-6387

MONTANA
Bureau of Records and Statistics
State Department of Health and
   Environmental Sciences
P.O. Box 200901
Helena, MT 59620-0901
(406) 444-2614

NEBRASKA
Bureau of Vital Statistics
State Department of Health
P.O. Box 95007
Lincoln, NE 68509-5007
(402) 471-2871

NEVADA
Office of Vital Statistics
505 East King Street
Carson City, NV 89710
(702) 687-4480

NEW HAMPSHIRE
Bureau of Vital Records
6 Hazen Drive
Concord, NH 03301-6527
(603) 271-4654

NEW JERSEY
State Department of Health
Bureau of Vital Statistics
CN-370
Trenton, NJ 08625
(609) 292-4087

NEW MEXICO
Bureau of Vital Records
1190 St. Francis Drive
P.O. Box 26110
Santa Fe, NM 87502
(505) 827-2338

NEW YORK (except New York City)
Bureau of Public Records
State Department of Health
Empire State Plaza
Tower Building
Albany, NY 12237
(518) 474-3075

NEW YORK CITY
Bureau of Vital Records
Department of Health of
    New York City
P.O. Box 3776
Church Street Station
New York, NY 10007
(212) 619-4530

NORTH CAROLINA
Department of Human Resources
Division of Health Services
Vital Records Branch
P.O. Box 29537
Raleigh, NC 27626
(919) 733-3526

NORTH DAKOTA
Division of Vital Records
State Department of Health
Office of Statistical Services
600 East Blvd.
Bismarck, ND 58505-0200
(701) 224-2360

OHIO
Bureau of Vital Statistics
State Department of Health
P.O. Box 15098
Columbus, OH 43215-0098
(614) 466-2531

OKLAHOMA
Vital Records Section
State Department of Health
P.O. Box 53551
Oklahoma City, OK 73152
(405) 271-4040

OREGON
Oregon State Health Division
Vital Records
P.O. Box 14050
Portland, OR 97214
(503) 731-4095

PENNSYLVANIA
Division of Vital Records
State Department of Health
P.O. Box 1528
New Castle, PA 16103
(412) 656-3100

RHODE ISLAND
Division of Vital Statistics
State Health Department
Room 101, 3 Capitol Hill
Providence, RI 02908-5097
(401) 277-2811

SOUTH CAROLINA
Office of Vital Records and Public
    Health Statistics
Department of Health and
    Environmental Control
2600 Bull Street
Columbia, SC 29201
(803) 734-4830

SOUTH DAKOTA
State Department of Health
Center for Health Policy
    and Statistics
Vital Records
445 East Capitol
Pierre, SD 57501-3185
(605) 773-3355

TENNESSEE
Office of Vital Records
Tennessee Department of Health
3rd Floor, Tennessee Tower
Nashville, TN 37247-0350
(615) 741-1763

TEXAS
Bureau of Vital Statistics
Texas Department of Health
1100 West 49th Street
Austin, TX 78756-3191
(512) 458-7111

UTAH
Bureau of Vital Records
Utah Department of Health
288 North 1480 West
P.O. Box 16700
Salt Lake City, UT 84116-0700
(801) 538-6105

VERMONT
Vermont Department of Health
Vital Records
P.O. Box 70
Burlington, VT 05402
(802) 863-7275

VIRGINIA
Division of Vital Records
State Health Department
P.O. Box 1000
Richmond, VA 23208-1000
(804) 786-6228

WASHINGTON
Center for Health Statistics
Vital Records
P.O. Box 9709
Olympia, WA 98507-9709
(206) 753-5936

WEST VIRGINIA
Vital Registration Office
State Capitol Complex
Building 3, Room 516
Charleston, WV 25305
(304) 558-2931

WISCONSIN
Section of Vital Records
Wisconsin Division of Health
P.O. Box 309
Madison, WI 53701
(608) 266-1371

WYOMING
Vital Records Services
Division of Health and Medical
   Services
Hathaway Building
Cheyenne, WY 82002
(307) 777-7591

SO MUCH TO DO, SO LITTLE TIME

B.C.: BEFORE CONCEPTION

- ❑ Begin financial planning; review health insurance coverage and maternity benefits.
- ❑ If necessary, buy health insurance, paying special attention to the date when pregnancy will be covered.

GETTING STARTED

MONTH 1 (OR BEFORE)

- ❑ Select a doctor or midwife:
  - • Get recommendations;
  - • Check credentials;
  - • Interview prospective doctors or midwives;
  - • Find out where your prospective health-care professionals have staff privileges;
  - • Make your selection.
- ❑ Decide where to have your baby: A hospital? A birthing center? At home?
  - • Review the list of facilities where your prospective doctors or midwives deliver babies;

- Visit the facilities if the location of where you would like to deliver plays a major role in determining who will deliver your baby;
- Select a facility.

☐ Again consult with the insurance company to clarify which specific procedures during pregnancy are covered.

MONTH 4

☐ Review the maternity/paternity policy at your workplace(s).

TIME FOR DECISIONS

MONTH 5

☐ Plan your will:
- Estimate your net worth;
- Plan the distribution of your assets;
- Make an appointment with an attorney;
- Select an executor and get his or her approval.

☐ Select a guardian:
- Select a guardian of the person and a guardian of the estate;
- Make sure the guardian is willing to serve.

☐ Assess your life insurance needs:
- Estimate the amount of insurance you need;
- Decide what kind of policy you need.

MONTH 6

☐ Draft your will:
- Meet with an attorney and draft your will;
- Draft a durable power of attorney;
- Draft a living will;
- Write a letter of final instructions.

☐ Inform your guardian of your child-rearing wishes:
- Write a letter of parental guidance for your guardian.

□ Evaluate life insurance options:
  - Collect estimates from four or five life insurance companies.

MONTH 7

□ Execute your will:
  - Complete your will;
  - Store it in a safe place.
□ Buy life insurance:
  - Purchase the best of the policies you have reviewed;
  - Store the policy in a safe place.
□ Prepare for your hospital stay:
  - Take childbirth classes;
  - Review your insurance coverage to make sure you understand the coverage and procedures;
  - Estimate your out-of-pocket health-care expenses.
□ Prepare for the homecoming:
  - Arrange for child care for your other children, if any;
  - Arrange for nursing care or assistance, if necessary when you arrive home from the hospital;
  - Buy or borrow furniture and equipment;
  - Interview prospective pediatricians.

FINISHING TOUCHES

MONTH 8

□ Prepare for your hospital stay:
  - Preregister at the hospital;
  - Notify your insurance company and get a precertification number, if necessary;
  - Investigate household help (cooking, cleaning, laundry, etc.), if you plan on hiring help.

MONTH 9

□ You're ready and waiting!

BIRTH

- ❑ Get a birth certificate.
- ❑ Apply for a Social Security card.
- ❑ Notify your insurance company about the birth and add your child to the policy.
- ❑ Keep careful records of your health care and expenses.
- ❑ Obtain an itemized bill from the hospital.
- ❑ File health insurance claims.
- ❑ If necessary, select child care:
  - Decide on the type of care;
  - Visit sites/interview candidates;
  - Select a facility/hire an individual;
  - If you hire an at-home worker, file the necessary paperwork for taxes, Social Security, unemployment, etc.
- ❑ Establish and contribute to a college savings fund.

ANNUAL REVIEW

- ❑ Review your life insurance needs. (Consider doing the review each time you write a check for your annual premiums.)
- ❑ Review your will. Have circumstances changed that merit any changes in your will?
- ❑ Review your choice of guardian. Is your first choice still the best choice?
- ❑ Consider new investments to reduce your tax bite.
- ❑ Review your college savings strategy; amend as needed.

WHEN YOUR CHILD REACHES AGE 14

- ❑ Begin to make changes in your college fund investments to take advantage of the tax laws. Begin to transfer the money into liquid assets that will be available to spend for college when the time comes.

INDEX

ABOUT THE AUTHOR

WINIFRED CONKLING writes for numerous national publications; she specializes in the topics of personal finance, consumer issues, and health. Before beginning a career as a free-lance writer, she was a writer and editor at *Consumer Reports* magazine and a newspaper reporter. She lives with her husband, Jonathan Rak, and her daughter Hannah Pamelia Rak, in Vienna, Virginia.